Accepting
Ourselves

Accepting Ourselves

*The Twelve-Step Journey
of Recovery
from Addiction
for Gay Men and Lesbians*

Sheppard B. Kominars

PERENNIAL LIBRARY

HARPER & ROW, PUBLISHERS,
SAN FRANCISCO
New York, Grand Rapids, Philadelphia, St. Louis
London, Singapore, Sydney, Tokyo

Library of Congress Cataloging-in-Publication Data

Kominars, Sheppard B.
    Accepting ourselves.

    Bibliography: p.
    1. Gays—United States—Alcohol use. 2. Alcoholics—
Rehabilitation—United States. 3. Alcoholism
counseling—United States. I. Title.
HV5139.K66 1989   362.2'92'0880664   88-45983
ISBN 0-06-250494-0
ISBN 0-06-250493-2 (pbk.)

89 90 91 92 93 MPC 10 9 8 7 6 5 4 3 2 1

To the survivors of addiction,
and to the children of the survivors,
especially Kathryn, Hugh and Matthew,
from their father

A survivor's testimony is more important than anything that can be written about survivors. It's important for them, important for the world. And for me, that is the most rewarding thing—to free, to open up the survivors. They live clandestinely. What made their being most unique was something they hid. That is most tragic—to suffer and then to suffer for having suffered.

—ELIE WIESEL

CONTENTS

ACKNOWLEDGMENTS

One of the great gifts of my recovery is my feeling of gratitude for my life and for the lives and experiences of others around me. Men and women throughout the United States, gay men, lesbians and heterosexuals, in and out of Twelve-Step programs, professionals in the field of addiction and the helping professions, friends, and family offered their help in reviewing and commenting on this manuscript. A few preferred to remain anonymous. They all spent many hours to help make this book as useful and inclusive as possible. I wish to thank Vivien Larsen for her love and support both in my own recovery over the past decade and in the editing of this book. I am deeply grateful for the comments and suggestions made by Louis Morales, Robert Kajdan, David Azzolina, Ben Gardiner, George Stevens, Mimi Goodwin, Peter Wiley, Jack Richard, Arthur Lingoursky, M.D., Corey Weinstein, M.D., and my daughter, Kathryn Kominars.

And for the care, thoughtfulness and love with which each chapter was edited and re-edited, I wish to thank my friend and partner in recovery, Marv Appelbaum, whose support over these past three years has changed my life in every way.

INTRODUCTION

I've written this book to encourage and support gay men, lesbians and their families in coming to a deeper acceptance of the problems that affect alcoholics and addicts* and of the process of recovery from addiction. Chemical dependency is a major crisis in the United States: one person in ten is an alcoholic. In the gay and lesbian community, the incidence of alcoholism and addiction is significantly higher—three in ten! Books to specifically address the predicament of the homosexual recovering from alcoholism and other addictions are long overdue. I know that my own journey in recovery, which began in 1980, would have been less difficult with this kind of support.

In *Accepting Ourselves,* I hope to provide a deeper understanding of certain conditions that many gay men and lesbians, for most of their lives, have denied or minimized. To accept ourselves without any intellectual understanding of what we are accepting keeps us always off balance, always at the mercy of the next assault. A road map that is written *for* gay and lesbian alcoholics can provide an experience-based context and perspective for the process of healing that is necessary in recovery.

In a normal, healthy growth process, the individual searches for knowledge and understanding. Wanting to belong, to be part of society, many homosexuals deny their homosexuality to the world (and often even to themselves); wanting to recover from addiction, homosexuals need support, intellectual as well as emotional, to advance

---

*Throughout this book, I use the terms *alcoholic* and *addict* interchangeably to refer to people suffering from alcoholism and/or other addictions. Either condition may be intended when either word appears in the text.

the process of acceptance of their sexuality. Gay and lesbian substance abusers who have already begun the recovery process are constantly looking for material to provide them with a sense of safety and self-identification in the midst of their struggle.

Gay men and lesbians who live in large cities with specifically identified gay and lesbian Twelve-Step meetings in each of the various recovery programs, have extensive possibilities for developing support groups to encourage the process. Those who live far from these centers, and those whose lives are painfully closeted, have need for additional kinds of perspective and support. With this book, I hope to provide an understanding and understandable companion in times of discouragement and stress.

Many parents, spouses, children, and friends of gay and lesbian substance abusers, both those in other Twelve-Step programs like Al-Anon and Adult Children of Alcoholics, and those who have not yet found any of these support systems, often suffer from some form of "alcohomophobia"—fear of the gay alcoholic. For their own recovery, they need to better understand the predicament of their loved one as well as the efforts they can make to focus on their own well-being. I've written *Accepting Ourselves* to provide them with a different perspective, one by which they can participate positively in the recovery process instead of continuing to suffer from either guilt over the past or fear of the future.

Those who work with addicted gay men and lesbians may also find this book helpful. Though it is not written specifically for health care givers with gay clients, it does present useful information about the experience and perspective of those who have come to them for help.

Anyone, gay or not, who is concerned with addiction and the process of recovery will find insights useful in understanding this journey. I have often seen reflected in the mirror of someone else's experience what I needed most to know about myself. *Accepting Ourselves* explores the learning process through which individuals become active participants in their own recovery and freedom.

More than eight years ago, I began my own recovery from substance abuse, and that experience lies at the center of this book. For more than twenty years, I was married and lived with my wife and three children. In 1976, after I was almost killed in a freak accident, I began using drugs and alcohol to anesthetize the pain from my injury. I became addicted without even realizing it, and I left my family in order to live and work in Puerto Rico, where I planned to end my life when my condition became too unbearable. Through an intervention beyond my understanding, I began to keep a journal in 1977, and as I wrote, some remarkable insights about recovery and what it would mean to live a whole and happy life appeared on the page.

My addiction progressed, however; in the meantime, several ideas germinated as well. In 1980, while collecting material for a film about the collapse of family life, I was invited to several meetings in which people talked about their addiction to alcohol and drugs and what they were doing about it. Through these meetings, I gradually became aware that I was dying not from the accident itself but from the effects of the substances I had been using. Writing in my journal had focused my attention on the reality of my predicament, and the meetings I began to attend started me on the steps of recovery into a sober life.

The first thing I had to accept was that, in fact, I had become addicted to alcohol and drugs. The second was that my recovery depended on accepting responsibility for being gay and coming out of the closet in which I had hidden as a married man. In developing the ideas I set forth in this book, I used both these crucial decisions as a foundation; both were necessary to sustain a program of recovery.

For the past six years, I have presented workshops on Homophobia, Risk-taking, and Creativity in Sobriety for gay men and lesbians in recovery in Philadelphia, Boston, Chicago, Portland, Oakland and San Francisco. Feedback from these presentations has provided a rich source of material.

I have worked as a counselor and facilitator in recovery groups in hospitals and halfway houses, and I have served as a consultant on the Episcopal Bishop of Pennsylvania's Special Subcommittee on Alcoholism and Substance Abuse. Having lived in urban centers where gay and lesbian addiction programs function actively, I have met a broad cross-section of gay men and lesbians in recovery and have close associations with straight, gay and lesbian therapists working in the field of substance abuse.

Accepting Ourselves is a how-to book, with ideas, suggestions and insights about the recovery process through which gay and lesbian alcoholics are living. It is a guide to what works. There are many ways to pursue the path of recovery; however, certain efforts take us further along the road than others. I hope to provide support and encouragement to attempt certain approaches and also to endorse the idea that we give ourselves permission, daily, to make as many mistakes as we need to make.

In writing this book, I have thought a great deal about the use of certain words. Through language, the currency of our value system, we exchange both the gold of ideas and the dross of prejudice and repression. The way in which you and I say things to each other can either enhance or diminish the quality of our lives. Therefore, I have made an effort to use words that will encourage lesbians and gay men to discover help and support for their recovery. I have consistently referred to each in the text so that neither would feel lost or left out. The effect may be repetitious, but I believe it is far more important to explicitly include rather than risk excluding anyone for whom this work is intended.

In this same spirit of using language to extend ideas instead of limiting them with sexist connotation, I have referred to God as either God or Higher Power, rather than He or She (except where quoting directly from AA literature). It would surprise me if "inclusive language" came as a shock for those who regularly attend religious services. My hope is to encourage readers who are used to this practice (and those who are not) to consider the ideas and experiences presented here without blocking themselves from connecting with the spiritual aspects of the journey into recovery.

It is not my intention to compromise anyone's personal beliefs. Those who consider themselves nonbelievers, atheists, or agnostics, and others who begin recovery after years of separation from any church or religion need to know that the belief in a power greater than oneself is not a condition for participation in a program of recovery. Willingness to begin the journey is more important than anything else, and the way is open to everyone.

Another major issue, the AIDS crisis and its impact on the homosexual community, has been very much in my thoughts as I wrote. I know many people with AIDS and HIV-positive tests who have used the Twelve Steps to deal with the emotional devastation they experience as addicted individuals. There can be no doubt that the Steps are invaluable tools to explore and expand the experience of living and coping with crisis. Exploring the Steps and their application to AIDS patients and those with HIV-positive tests would require an entire book, however. For this reason, I decided to keep the focus directly upon gay men and lesbians suffering from addiction in all conditions of health.

The process of recovering from addiction involves the physical, the emotional, the intellectual and the spiritual. *Accepting Ourselves* addresses these crucial areas of recovery: repairing the body; restoring emotional balance; and developing an intimate connection with a spiritual source beyond oneself. We prepare for a healthy life through careful attention to *each* of these areas, and we need to be alert to the danger of replacing one addiction with another (e.g., food for alcohol, sex for drugs, etc.). Switching addictions is very common for anyone who is recovering; by paying attention to each of these areas, we can diminish the possibility of this occurring.

At the heart of all of the Twelve-Step programs are the paradoxes: "Surrender to win," "You've got to give it away in order to keep it," and others. In my own life, it was only when I came closest to dying that I became willing to face the prospect of living differently. This same experience has been true for countless others who have found their way into recovery.

Change is confusing and terrifying, and in order to embark upon it, the individual must enter a state of willingness. The paradox of death in life is well known to the addict, and contemplating suicide as a way out of his or her anguish is something many homosexuals can identify with. *Accepting Ourselves* will develop the significant role of these paradoxes as it explores the pathway to progress in recovery.

Accepting Ourselves uses the Twelve Steps of the recovery programs based on Alcoholics Anonymous. Each chapter will explore the addictive condition from which the gay or lesbian alcoholic is suffering, then present the alternative(s) in recovery. Until we are clear about any condition that needs to be changed, we have no reason for embracing an alternative! Linking them together, it is possible to find a way through the maze of our predicament when we first confront the possibility of abstaining from the use of substances. Instead of remaining stuck in the condition, instead of allowing the condition to continue to overwhelm us, we can consider what it might be like to live without it. Focusing on the alternatives, we can then begin to work at recovery in a practical and meaningful way. These are the twelve conditions and the twelve alternatives we are offered in recovery:

Condition	Alternatives
1. Denial	Acceptance
2. Isolation and fear	Faith or belief
3. Willful powerlessness	Willing, positive action
4. Self-delusion	Self-revelation
5. Repression and/or stagnation	Cleansing and renewal
6. Inflexibility	Flexibility
7. Arrogance	Humility
8. Irresponsibility	Responsibility
9. Suffering and fragmentation	Healing and fusion
10. Backsliding	Self-discipline
11. Self-centeredness	Spiritual bonding
12. Self-seeking	Communion and service

Because the process of recovery is very slow, we move into each of these areas in different parts of our lives a little at a time. Working continually through the cycle of the Twelve Steps never fails to reveal new areas for recovery, no matter how far along we are in the process. *Accepting Ourselves* explores the route of the journey and provides a balanced perspective for the novice and the veteran traveler of any age. Many of us know the place we start from, but none of us know how far we will go along the way. For all of us, recovery is the greatest adventure of our lives, and we each reach far beyond anything we ever knew or expected with every step we take.

This book is a map of a journey, with guides to progress: stories about recovery, suggestions for action, and reflections to encourage the traveler along the way. I am still walking the path, and I pray each day for the patience, humility, courage and persistence to continue. I invite every reader who wishes to share the experience of reading and using this book to write to me in care of the publisher. Your thoughts will be of particular interest and value to me both in future writing and for my own journey into the future.

THE TWELVE STEPS OF
ALCOHOLICS ANONYMOUS

Step One: We admitted we were powerless over alcohol—
             that our lives had become unmanageable.

Step Two: Came to believe that a Power greater than
             ourselves could restore us to sanity.

Step Three: Made a decision to turn our will and our lives
             over to the care of God *as we understood Him.*

Step Four: Made a searching and fearless moral inventory
             of ourselves.

Step Five: Admitted to God, to ourselves, and to another
             human being the exact nature of our wrongs.

Step Six: Were entirely ready to have God remove all
             these defects of character.

Step Seven: Humbly asked Him to remove our
             shortcomings.

Step Eight: Made a list of all persons we had harmed, and
             became willing to make amends to them all.

Step Nine: Made direct amends to such people wherever
             possible except when to do so would injure
             them or others.

Step Ten: Continued to take personal inventory and
             when we were wrong promptly admitted it.

Step Eleven: Sought through prayer and meditation to
             improve our conscious contact with God *as we
             understood Him,* praying only for knowledge of
             His will for us and the power to carry that
             out.

Step Twelve: Having had a spiritual awakening as the result
             of these steps, we tried to carry this message
             to alcoholics, and to practice these principles
             in all our affairs.

From *Alcoholics Anonymous,* 3rd Ed. (New York: Alcoholics Anonymous World Services, 1976), 59–60. Reprinted here and throughout this work by permission from A.A. World Services, Inc.

Step One

THE PARADOX OF DENIAL

CONDITION: DENIAL

How natural it is to wish to turn our backs on anything we do not like about ourselves! For as long as we can, we get away with it. We encourage family, lovers and friends, employers and strangers to help us go on believing we are the way we'd like to be instead of the way we are. When we can no longer avoid looking at the effects of alcohol or other substances on our lives, we come face to face with our denial. For some people, this means "hitting bottom." As long as we pretend that we are not dependent on the addictions that run our lives, we are in denial.

ALTERNATIVE: ACCEPTANCE

By accepting ourselves as we are—gay and lesbian alcoholics— we can begin to recover from addiction.

STEP ONE:

We admitted we were powerless over alcohol and other mood-altering substances—that our lives had become unmanageable.

Beginning recovery as a lesbian or gay man means that wherever we start the journey, the road is forged through peaks and abysses known only to us. I know this is true from my own experience and from the stories of other people. Sharing this journey of recovery as simply and honestly as possible will be my task, and I begin with the hope that it will provide others with the strength and support they need on their way into a new life.

It is especially difficult for straight men and women, both those recovering from addiction and others who are not at risk, to understand what it is like for lesbians and gay men who set out on the journey of recovery. The answer to the question, Isn't recovery the same for everyone, gay or straight, lesbian or gay? is yes *and* no. We need to appreciate and respond to the differences.

The description of the journey starts with my own story, for that is where recovery begins—with the individual. Between 1985 and 1987, I wrote a novel about hitting bottom in my addiction and beginning a new life. Writing that book was, in a lifetime of high-wired, acrobatic risks, the greatest risk I have ever taken. Through the eyes of a writer setting down his own story, I developed a sense of purpose that I had spent many years avoiding. The effort to describe what had happened brought me into an intimate relationship with the man I have become.

Fortunately for me, instead of living my story over again—living *in* my story, the way so many others do—I began to live *through* all that had happened instead of being lost to it. I was no longer stuck in the past but enriching the present with my own experience. My life began to belong to me in some new and authentic way; gone was the old feeling of everything being painfully accidental. It was a breakthrough.

Alcoholism, addiction to a substance, has been called the disease of denial. It is one of the few diseases that tells you you do not have a disease. In fact, the presence of denial is one of the surest clues that the disease is at work. Though others may be able to recognize the evidence, denial will make it impossible for those who suffer to see the symptoms in themselves. How insidious! Alcoholism *is* insidious, along with being cunning, baffling and powerful enough to destroy the lives of everyone it touches.

The autobiographical novel I wrote relates the destructive process of addiction in the life of a successful executive and his family. He begins in denial. After years of pretending to live happily in the little house on the river with a beautiful wife, adoring children, and a comfortable income, he is seriously injured in a car accident, and his life becomes a nightmare of pain and despair.

In his flight into isolation, drugs and alcohol, he encounters the self he thought he left behind. He is overwhelmed by the experience of falling in love with another man. He sinks further and further into addiction as he denies his love, and he prepares to commit suicide. This is a story that many people have experienced firsthand: denial kills.

The man in that story shares a trait common to all addicts: denial that he's an alcoholic. Compound this condition with the denial of our sexuality, and we raise the destructive power of addiction to the maximum. In the early stages of recovery, it is common for gay men or lesbians to drink or use drugs again and again because of being unable to accept being homosexual. In addiction, many of us have found it possible to endure intense pressure and strain; in sobriety, there is no mood-altering substance to deaden these feelings. Even those who thought they had completely accepted their sexuality are often startled to discover old doubts and fears again staring them in the face once they stop drinking. They find they need to begin the acceptance process all over again.

The Bar Scene

Unlike the man in the novel who was completely closeted, many gay men and lesbians, in the normal course of their lives, spend a great deal of time in bars or discos. The gay bar is frequently the center of activity and recreation for both couples and singles. Bars and discos are a place to hang out, meet friends, find new partners, and, in general, relax and enjoy life. A party in someone's home is a special occasion; a night at the bar is any night of the week. Gay life, for those new to it, is often focused on the bar scene.

For many of us, the bars at first seemed glamorous and exciting compared with the lives we lived at home in our families. There were new faces, people to talk to, and the kind of stimulation we had been looking for. The bars were the place to be. As time passed, however, and as the scene grew more and more familiar, a feeling of routine set in. When the glamour fades and boredom begins, the alcohol in the glass assumes a different role: it becomes the real reason why we go to the bar. But by then the habit is so natural that the truth is almost impossible to recognize.

Many gay men and lesbians may identify with this monologue I remember so vividly after going to the bars for several years:

Guess I'm up for a little change of scenery tonight. I'm tryin' out a different bar. At least the name out front is different. Still looks like all the others inside. I'll see if I can get one of those stools at the end of the bar. Damn! That nerd just changed his mind and ordered another drink instead of leaving. What's the matter, doesn't he have a home? If I'd gone to my usual place, I'd have a seat by now. Then again, maybe I wouldn't.

The bunch drinking here look and sound just like the people in my usual hangout; haven't I seen them all before? Everyone's beginning to look alike to me. That phony kind of cheery sullenness (or is it sullen cheeriness?) is every place I go. And the music they pipe in from the sound system is like sticky icing on a stale birthday cake. The whole scene is stale. I should know, I've lived it night after night! Why do I keep telling myself it's the place to have fun? Can't understand it!

But I'm here. Where else do I have to go? I'll order another drink. I didn't drive all the way downtown just to turn around and drive home! Look at that—I was wrong about the other guy, but the one on my left is on his way to the door. Now that feels good: to be perched up here in my favorite spot on a bar stool. How about another drink? Sure. Isn't that what livin' right is all about?

Variations on this monologue are endless, but the basic condition is the same: we find ourselves trapped inside the bottle with no place else to go. What happened to all the good times? The good times now are rare, even though we never give up searching for them, and we compensate for our disappointment by losing ourselves in booze and drugs. What began in fun becomes an absolute necessity; we cannot live without it. Without any warning, we become addicted, and the progress of the disease accelerates undetected. We are hooked, and we don't even know it.

How Can I Tell?

Several years ago, I met Paul, who had just come out of the hospital after suffering severe depression brought on by excessive use of alcohol and drugs. The previous spring, he had been hospitalized after an auto accident in which he had almost been killed. His use of alcohol before the car crash had never been a problem—except for bad hangovers when he really overdid it. Paul had a very hard time believing he had become an alcoholic. He went to a few AA meetings to find out how people knew whether or not they were alcoholics. An old-timer named John told him this:

Try this program for ninety days: don't drink alcohol or use any other drugs for ninety days. If you really don't have a problem, everything will be fine.

For some reason he couldn't explain, Paul decided to try it—just to see what happened. To his absolute horror, he discovered he couldn't get through even three days without drinking, let alone ninety!

Paul's story isn't too different from mine. Both of us thought that an auto accident had brought on our health crisis and caused our lives to become unmanageable. How could the alcohol that brought relief have taken over our minds and bodies? The explanation was quite simple: we had both used the drugs the doctors had prescribed, along with more alcohol, to anesthetize the physical pain and the emotional despair we felt. Slowly, a dose at a time, our systems had become dependent on these substances without our knowing it. After what we had already endured, each of us asked, "But why me? Why has such a thing happened to me?"

Every alcoholic has asked these same questions. The fact we face is shattering and incomprehensible. Our questions remind us of another appeal for an explanation: Why am I gay? Why am I lesbian? It is an enigma. There is only one response that has made any sense at all to me: "Why *not* me?"

Neither running away, nor hiding from anything, nor denial brings relief that lasts through the night. Though I may think I have escaped from everyone and everything, I find I am always alone with myself in the darkness between 3:00 and 4:00 a.m. My only hope for peace comes then in accepting myself exactly as I am.

"Why Me?"

The question, Why me? is at the heart of the alcoholic's denial system. Denial is the mask we use to protect ourselves from the reality, from the truth that we are addicted, that we are substance abusers, that we are hooked. By asking the question, the substance abuser masks the truth that it *is* he or she, and that IS the way it *is*. The question begs for a different answer.

I do not believe that anyone ever set out in life to be an alcoholic or an addict. It happened along the way. Addiction sets in as alcohol or other mood-altering substances gain control over our physical, emotional and mental systems. And in the place where things only happen, where we happen to something or it happens to us, we function as victims. As victims, there is no help for us. We are only there to be victimized.

In our denial, in our nonacceptance of the man or woman we are, other people intentionally, as well as thoughtlessly, negate who we are and all that we value and act on. Living as a negative entity in a positive world is the predicament of the gay man or lesbian who does not accept himself or herself *and* of the alcoholic who does not accept that he or she is an alcoholic. Living like this is living in a nightmare.

In this bad dream, the world is upside down; suffering is a source of pleasure. As perverse as it sounds, alcoholics find in suffering, in their addiction, something positive. The alcoholic is addicted to pain and suffering; the victim is addicted to pain and suffering. Denial makes it possible for this upside-down world to function. We do not have to search very far for the reason. As gay men and lesbians, we have been conditioned in our homes, our schools, our churches—everywhere in our society—to be victims and to deny what is, and to accept what is not. Under these circumstances, it is little wonder that gay men and lesbians are at such a high risk for addiction.

Many people know about the risk; nevertheless, they choose to believe it can never happen to *them*. It looms as too big a threat. The moment their upside-down world becomes shaky, they implement every defense they can think of: "I am too intelligent!" "I'm too rich (or too poor)!" "I'm too young!" "I only drink beer!" "The doctor prescribed it!" "It couldn't happen to me!" "My life isn't unmanageable; I don't live in the gutter!" Their defenses are legion, but all are actually forms of denial. For most substance abusers, it takes a special kind of personal calamity like a serious accident, loss of a job, breakup of a relationship, or a devastating medical diagnosis to come face to face with the truth: "I am an alcoholic." "I am an addict."

No one can make another person say this and *mean* it; the addict is the only one who can do it. One may feel enormous pain in getting to a point where such an admission is possible, but the relief of being able to do it is indescribable. With those four words, the way is opened for us to receive help. Until that moment, we are isolated by addiction and cut off from hope. Why is that? The disease masks itself with many different disguises—as many as one out of three hospital beds may be filled by patients with complications arising from substance abuse. Until the individual treats the root cause of his or her problems, the complications go on multiplying.

Accepting that "I am an alcoholic" is the beginning of the process of dealing with the unmanageable life of addiction. It's as simple as that. Then why is it so incredibly difficult for a gay man or lesbian to accept it? It is through alcohol, through mood-altering substances, that so many of us found (we believed) the comfort and acceptance that was missing in our lives. How can we live without these "friends" who have seen us through the night? Where, after all, is there to go? Our loneliness and our isolation from society is real. Is this void, then, the alternative to drinking and using? It is no surprise that the drunk gives in to addiction without a second thought: "I couldn't stand living without alcohol or drugs, so don't even suggest it!"

An Agonizing Choice

Alone or in relationships, gay men and lesbians face an agonizing choice. Drugs and alcohol are often at the center of the connection with lovers, as well as friends. The prospect of breaking up—as unhealthy or painful as the relationship might be because of substance abuse—is as terrifying as leaving the bars for those who make them the focus of their social and "family" life. Putting up with bad is at least better than *disaster,* and many are willing to settle for that.

Straight men and women, when they first abstain from alcohol and substances, are painfully in touch with the bitter experience of isolation that has built up between them and the rest of society during their addiction. For gay men, for lesbians, who already suffer from the isolation separating us from society, that is a double dose of despair to swallow. In a society that deprives homosexuals of their human rights and ostracizes them for their basic human desire to relate with others like themselves, there seems no place to turn. Discriminated against on the basis of sexual preference, gay men and women face the devastating prospect of being discriminated against as alcoholics *as well*. Remembering that it was through alcohol that life became a little less difficult to bear, denial often seems the only choice possible.

Alcoholism, addiction to any substance, is a disease of denial. What needs to be added is that, for many who suffer from the disease, becoming addicted was the only way to stay sane. The choice to drink or to use was what made it possible to put up with the cruelty and abuse, the hatred, the discrimination, the distortions of the truth that lesbians and gay men experience. Just like the actual alcohol and drugs, the denial of who we are as gay men and lesbians, the denial of our value as loving and responsible human beings entitled to live happy lives along with everyone else, made it possible to support the little there was left to settle for. Being hooked on denial made life at least a little more bearable.

But the least is far too little to settle for in a world in which every man and every woman has the responsibility of finding joy and happiness. When we become willing to look through the *other* end of the telescope at the "upside-down" world we settled for, we finally understand there is an alternative: acceptance—of ourselves exactly as we are, and of our task of finding joy and making our own unique contribution to life and the world around us. With such understanding, gay and lesbian alcoholics can appreciate that denial is unnatural and merely a symptom of the disease. It is then possible to recognize how denial, instead of being the basis for uniqueness, forces everyone who suffers from it to live like outcasts in a foreign land.

Accepting Our Denial

Accepting denial is the beginning of recovery, because when we no longer have to live in opposition to denial, its force and persistence diminish. When denial loses its power, other alternatives appear. We may have little or no idea what living a different kind of life might mean, but we can begin to understand that the way we've been living does not have to continue. It takes a long time for many of us to reach this place. We have been looking through the wrong end of the telescope for so long that we are capable only of tunnel vision— until some shock powerful enough occurs in our lives.

For me, it was a freak auto accident; for others, it was another kind of shock that accelerated the unmanageability of their lives, sent them spinning downward into the vortex of self-destruction. Quickly or slowly, we hit bottom, and it is a different place for each of us. Continual denial that we are alcoholics pushes us to lower and lower bottoms. There comes a time, however, when we are either sick enough or frightened enough or desperate enough to say, "No further! I'm getting off here!" Or, "I'm sick and tired of being sick and tired!"

I once heard this called "Step Zero: This shit has got to stop!" It is the moment, the bottom, from which recovery begins. Accepting that one is in such a place, no matter how little or how much one has lost, is the only way it is possible to receive help.

There is an interesting similarity between "coming out of the closet" as gay men or lesbians and accepting ourselves as alcoholics. Both acts admit there is a real life to live outside of isolation and despair, and that the choice to live it is ours. In the closet, gay men and lesbians pretend they are *not* this or *not* that. What a difference to be able to say: I *am* this, I *am* that! This is an act of affirmation; it carries with it basic human entitlements instead of rejection and scorn. Affirmation is power, and with power now directed back to its very source—ourselves—instead of being given away to others, we begin the process of living a healthy life that no longer has to be lived "upside down." Coming out of the closet makes it possible for us to live in the world as a positive force instead of a negative one.

This is exactly the courage that is essential if we are to accept ourselves as being alcoholics. I will never forget the first time I said the words out loud. Sitting on the terrace on a Sunday morning in Isla Verde, Puerto Rico, I thought my whole world was going to collapse. But instead of collapsing, by accepting myself as addicted, I made it possible to receive the help I needed to begin recovery into life. The act itself was incredibly difficult for me. Nevertheless, the fact was very simple: affirmation is the end to denial. Affirmation opens the way into one's own life again.

As a victim, one cannot make such a transformation, and that is the best explanation for why change cannot begin unless gay and lesbian alcoholics accept themselves as alcoholics. What makes us truly different from one another is the way in which each of us uses our energy. Denial deprives us of energy and forces us to live as victims. Acceptance, by contrast, initiates responsible action.

No one else can do this for us. We are the only ones who can accept ourselves. Indeed, others can show us how they have done it for themselves, but unless we do it for ourselves, we must live in denial—with the world upside down. Acceptance is the only gift from the sea of recovery that we can give ourselves. That is why it is so difficult to grasp! Once we do, however, others can help us.

Many gay men and lesbians have grown up in a world in which shame and scorn are daily experiences. They are not in the habit of affirming themselves; they are not in the habit of trusting others to affirm them. Imagine how difficult it is, therefore, to believe that the solution to problems is not in the bottle, and that there are others who *can* help us! Living in an upside-down world, we have told ourselves that we *cannot* be gay and happy and sober; that's the message society has given us. We can never discover this is a lie until we begin to live the truth. Taking the first step of self-acceptance is an incredible risk, but one that opens a new way of living. It is this risk that many have balked at, thinking that they, in their own uniqueness, could find an easier, softer way.

Gay and lesbian alcoholics often fool themselves into believing it is fear of something, or someone, or the past, *instead of their disease,* that makes them hang on to their addiction or that drives them back into using again. In addiction, we *know* exactly where we will end up; in sobriety, we have no idea, and that is why sobriety is such a risk. Sobriety is the real challenge, not addiction. Can we do it? Are we worth such a gift? Acceptance of ourselves as worthy comes only in the act itself, and the way to begin has already begun if you have read this far.

For those who doubt whether they are alcoholics or are involved with people who are, there are two lists of questions in appendix A and appendix B. Allow yourself the benefit of answering the questions honestly. You can do this for yourself. The rewards are waiting for you if you do, and the choice of receiving them is entirely yours. Not one gift from the sea of recovery will be withheld once you reach out for the first one: acceptance. Acceptance is the beginning of everything.

GUIDES TO PROGRESS

Sally was twenty-six and had never thought very much about the way she drank or the weird things that kept happening to her, such as waking up in strange beds or never being able to find her car after a night at a bar. As far as she was concerned, there was nothing unusual about being unable to remember whom she was sleeping with or where they had met. Her friend, Laura, gave her a pamphlet filled with questions about alcohol and the way she lived her life. Sally was really shocked by them! How could anyone know so much about her without even being there to see how she lived? "Even though it isn't pretty, it's not too late to do something about it," she admitted to Laura over dinner after her first AA meeting. This was Sally's breakthrough out of denial, and with it she began her entry into recovery.

Herb was forty eight and had lived his entire life in the closet. He often found himself bruised and sore the next morning after a night on the town. There were even times he woke up in his car in unfamiliar neighborhoods in distant suburbs. It was always the same story: after he took the first drink, he couldn't remember anything that happened to him. The idea of *not* taking the first drink had never occurred to him until he heard it from the intake counselor at the detox center where he woke up three years ago after a blackout. "It's not the fourth or fifth drink that gets you drunk; it's the first one!" Somehow, this got through to him, and a chink of light appeared in all the darkness. It was difficult to admit he was an alcoholic; it was even harder to admit that he was gay. It took him several years in mainstream AA before he was able to do this, and a whole new life opened when he did.

Suggestions for Action

After you have answered the questions in appendix A, consider how you feel about your life and your future. Do you want to continue exactly as before, or would you like to make some changes? Perhaps you know someone already in a Twelve-Step program with whom you could talk about addiction. Arrange to meet that person to discuss some of your concerns. Give yourself the opportunity to learn from others what they did to find help.

REFLECTIONS

As unique as any of us are, as addicts and alcoholics, we have in common a great deal of pain and suffering. As survivors, we also have much to be grateful for today.

THE DISEASE OF ISOLATION

CONDITION: ISOLATION AND FEAR

By ourselves or with other people, we have felt lonely and afraid. Perhaps we thought the bars and the discos would change all this. They didn't. If anything, we began to feel even lonelier and more frightened as time went on. Alcohol seemed to be the only thing that worked; it became our bosom buddy. We came to rely on it more and more—until we began to notice that we were becoming even more frightened and alone than before. We had drunk ourselves into a corner with nowhere to turn. Physically, emotionally and spiritually, we became desperate and hopeless.

ALTERNATIVE: FAITH OR BELIEF

The antidote to our disease is faith in a Power greater than ourselves. Developing this faith opens the way to help and hope.

STEP TWO:

Came to believe that a Power greater than ourselves could restore us to sanity.

Alcoholism is like an elevator ride to the bottom of the universe. At any stop along the way, addicts can get off if they make a conscious decision to get help. The most common response for gay and lesbian substance abusers is to insist that nothing bad has happened yet, so there is no reason to end the joy ride.

A few months ago, I listened as Nancy, a 22-year-old lesbian, became very indignant at the suggestion she might have a drinking problem. She spoke for many who do not want to consider getting off the elevator:

Listen, I'm not like those drunks! I've got a job; I've got an apartment; I've got a lover! Does that sound like someone who's hangin' on to the curb looking for the next drink?

Even though Nancy couldn't get through a day without a six-pack and several vodka and tonics, she hadn't *yet* experienced the full effects of alcohol dependency on her life. These three letters, *y e t,* are only the acronym for *You're Eligible Too.* If it hasn't happened yet, we can be certain that the rest will follow as the ride continues to the bottom.

Stepping Off the Down Elevator

Denial, as we have already seen, is a powerful force, and the evidence of *yet*—if it isn't too weighty—requires little effort to dismiss. There are many who must prove this to themselves, but there are a few who are willing to let this "research" be carried on by others. We are the lucky ones who get off the elevator before "yet" happens.

"Lucky" is hardly the way most people in their first few days without alcohol or drugs would describe themselves. The physical symptoms of withdrawal are painful and often require professional attention because of the danger of harm to the body. The body fights back to secure the "fix" it has been deprived of, and the mind and the emotions are willingly enlisted in this combat. It feels like living in no-man's-land on the battlefield; it is like being in a wilderness in which everything seems unreal except *my* pain, *my* confusion, *my* terror. I remember asking myself, "Is this why I stopped drinking?

Is this what putting down the alcohol and the drugs gets me? You've got to be kidding!"

During those initial days after deciding to find out what would happen if I stopped drinking, I could not understand what people did with their lives day and night without alcohol. It baffled me completely! Alcohol had become such an entrenched part of my routine that being without it seemed unnatural. I was lost, totally lost, without it. All sense of security vanished and, I was certain, would never return. One of the most frightening things alcoholics tell themselves when they are in a bad place is that it will *always* be like this—"I will never feel better again." We tell ourselves that unless we drink or use, we will die. In the wilderness, it is the voice we know the best, and it finds us any hour of the day or night.

The voice that tells us this does not speak the truth. It's our addiction that says to us, "You can't make it without *me!*" Without help, it is almost impossible to hear any other voice. As strange as it may seem, we are somehow able to listen to other addicts who tell us how *they* made it through this place and are still alive to talk about it.

The things I know best have to do with the stuff I'm using. I'm an expert on where to get it, the sources, the prices and the frequency. It took over my life. Everything I did was focused on my addiction. If someone can't understand this, then I can't trust him or her. That's why if I'm going to get through this no-man's-land, I've got to hear it from others just like myself who have done it. I've got to hear it from people who talk my language instead of doctors in white coats who talk in jargon only they can understand.

Some alcoholics I have known have put down the drink and "white-knuckled it" on their own. As far as they are concerned, they don't need anyone else to support their efforts to stay clean and sober. Except for not drinking, their lives have changed very little. Usually, the same compulsive behavior begins in other areas, like work, sex, relationships, or with other substances like cigarettes, pills, food. The pain starts all over in a new place.

Choices

In addiction, there are no choices: nothing will satisfy us except the substance on which we depend. In sobriety, in abstinence, we have an infinite variety of choices. One of them is choosing to participate in a Twelve-Step recovery program. In meetings, we can hear from others who have been in the same place before us, or who are there right now, exactly where we are. What a shock it is to discover others just like ourselves!

I am alone: I am *not* alone.

This is an amazing paradox; just when we believe we are totally alone, without a relationship or any of the friends from the bars or the crowd we used with, just when we find ourselves in the midst of the wilderness, we see men and women just like us at the gay AA meetings, the gay Narcotics Anonymous meetings, the gay Overeaters Anonymous meetings. Is this possible? Is there really life *outside* the bars for a gay man or a lesbian? Are there others who have left relationships centered on booze and drug dependency and survived? Can we live without the world upside down? Can we trade such a world for a life in this new wilderness?

These questions can be answered if we are willing to collect the data needed to support the evidence. We can begin by answering some questions about what life was really like at the bars.

- Except for the drink in my hand and the stool beneath me, how happy and comfortable was I from the minute I walked in until I left (assuming I can remember from beginning to end)?
- What about the people around me: how happy were they?
- What was actually happening to me most of the time I thought I was "having fun"?
- Was getting drunk all that great?
- What do I have to show for it?
- What kind of success did I have in finding someone to share my life? (Wasn't my primary relationship with alcohol, not other people?)
- What made me believe I couldn't live outside the bars or my habit?

Even as we begin looking at these questions, it is possible to see that we carefully surrounded ourselves with others like ourselves just to make certain we would never stop to ask such questions. What we all had in common was that we deluded ourselves and abused ourselves in the same ways! The proof of this is that we never allowed anyone who thought differently to get close to us.

The temptation to continue with the delusion and the abuse is very powerful in the early days of sobriety; it is a temptation to choose the "safety" of the world upside down over the hazards of life in the wilderness. Considering that we have been able to live our lives and establish some semblance of comfort with booze, this temptation appears to make a great deal of sense—until we review the evidence. The bar wasn't the place we thought it was. And we weren't the happy souls we thought we were, either. Is it just possible, now, that this wilderness in which we find ourselves isn't the place we think it is?

Experiencing ourselves as children, lost children, terribly uncertain and in need of help, we may begin to see how rigorously we supported our lives and defended ourselves against being in such a vulnerable state. It is also possible to see how this belief about being able to manage things in this upside-down condition actually prevented any change from occurring.

The Wilderness

What if the wilderness we're in is a place of growth, a place for change? Instead of being a setting in which the only alternative is to sit and pour alcohol and drugs into our systems to fill the void that has been eaten into us, perhaps in the wilderness we have the space and the time to get into action, real action. Perhaps it is a zone in which we can discover who we are and what we can do without the alcohol and the drugs to confuse us. In this place, we may just begin to be able to see our lives in a different way.

There is a line in the Talmud, a remarkable book of wisdom that has survived many centuries, that says, "I do not see the world the way it is, I see the world the way I am." As alcoholics, we see and live in a drunken, addicted world. In early sobriety, we are terribly disoriented; we lose almost everything familiar to us because we have stopped using the substances that made it all "intelligible." It will take time to create a new sense of order and familiarity, and in this wilderness we discover others, like ourselves, who are just as disoriented.

Our lives are the reflection of what we value. When we value things, we fill our lives with things; when we value people, we fill our lives with people. And when we begin to value sobriety, our lives begin to reflect a world very different from the one we knew before. Is it any wonder that we are dismayed and frightened?

At the Twelve-Step meetings in which others share their experience, we begin to receive glimmers of understanding about the isolated and isolating lives we lived. Instead of being a mark of our uniqueness, as we thought, we discover that isolation is but a symptom of our disease. Through the voices of others, we begin to hear things we have never heard another person speak of, things we never believed possible—except inside our own head. Listening to gay men and lesbians share their most intimate secrets, we hear the story of our own lives. That story is powerful; and we make a powerful identification with it.

For some of us, unless we can identify with the experience others share, we are unable to feel the power that passes through them to us. In straight meetings, lesbians and gay men may have to struggle to identify in some way with others in the room. They may find these meetings unsatisfying; they may even find their deep sense of isolation accentuated. For many of us, in order to feel the power, we must believe the speaker knows *our* suffering. Gay meetings have grown in number all over the world, and they have provided the opportunity to meet and hear others whose story—"her-story" and "his-story"— can be told in an environment of understanding and acceptance. Wherever and whenever we identify with someone's story, we transcend race and ethnicity and sexual orientation, and we are able to hear the whole message of recovery.

It may take months or years for some recovering addicts to find their way to a gay meeting. One aspect of isolation is "homophobia,"* and we must deal with this crucial issue in recovery. Gay meetings are of tremendous help in coming to grips with the complexity of how homophobia works in the lives of gay and lesbian alcoholics.

---

*Homophobia is the condition of general fear or uneasiness about homosexuality or behavior that is considered homosexual.

In our society, homophobia is the rule, not the exception. Children growing up with straight parents experience it whether they live in a warm and loving family or a loveless one. Little boys and girls are brought up with fears about "different" people, and they learn to shun feelings that in any way reflect sympathy or identification with "those kinds of people."

At the same time children learn to mistrust certain feelings in themselves, they begin to mistrust the parents who invalidate these feelings. It is not uncommon for children with gay or lesbian feelings, growing up in a straight household, to believe they don't belong there. They may even believe themselves to be adopted instead of the natural offspring of these adults who make lies out of their innocent, honest feelings. Having these basic feelings invalidated is one of the best reasons for mistrusting the source of invalidation.

It is also one of the best reasons for developing a highly judgmental, hypercritical attitude toward others: "If that is what they think about me, then this is what I think about *them*." Gay men and lesbians, having grown up in a homophobic society, are among the most critical people in the world. This is apparent in conversations about many subjects, especially other gay men and lesbians. As the best defense of their lifestyle, many have chosen to be critical of everyone and everything. Their defense is a first-attack offense.

It Begins with Sharing

At Twelve-Step meetings, instead of the criticism and one-upmanship that we are used to, we hear others share their stories about living as drunks and addicts. This has an unusual effect on us: we begin to identify with our own survival power as gay and lesbian alcoholics. The stories of others give us courage. With this courage, we begin to redirect our energy toward getting sober. Have we not spent years using our energy to hide the fact we were gay and lesbian? We are experts in secrecy and denial. But at the gay meetings, hearing others talk about it so openly, the way clears for us to begin to focus this previously misdirected energy on recovery.

Surrounded by others sharing their experience honestly in language so familiar and yet so different from the bar scene, we may sit silently for a while. It is not too long, however, before we participate in sharing bits and pieces of our own story. "If this is what it's like to feel lost and scared, I might as well put in my two cents!"

And the moment we share, in this wilderness, we come face to face with the realization that we are not alone. As we add our voice to the others, we hear in the sound we make together the power greater than ourselves that has always been there, ready and waiting for us to be available for help. The dead end that we reached was the effect of the substances we used and of growing up in a dysfunctional family; it was not because of our lack of entitlement in the human race, which is *both* gay and straight. In hitting bottom, we reach a place in which we discover that *we* are the ones who think of ourselves as isolated and completely alone. We are the reflection of our self-delusion: since things didn't work out the way we thought they should, we cut ourselves off from others, from the kind of connection and help that is available to us in life.

In the support that flows from the group, we find a strength that we never had on our own. Acknowledging the group acknowledges also the power that is there in all of us if we work together at the task of recovery. Sharing problems together reduces the magnitude of the problem for some reason, some miraculous reason. We come to this understanding, however, only when we have reached a place in ourselves where we are available to help. This, it is important to see, is not a condition of helplessness, because those who believe that they are helpless are *not* available for help. The person who is available to be helped is never helpless.

When we are available to be helped, we can then begin to believe there is help for us. We remain completely isolated for as long as we believe that we are helpless.

The delusion of the bar scene is that, in it, we felt we were normal, free to be ourselves without hiding, because there were other isolated people *just like us*. But we made no efforts, or few efforts, to make any real connections beyond escaping. With or without anyone else, we escaped into our loneliness. We medicated ourselves so that we would not feel the pain, and we came to trust the alcohol because it helped relieve the pain—until it became itself the source of the agony.

When the world turns around and is no longer upside down, the way out of feeling the pain is through allowing ourselves to feel it!

Instead of avoiding the feelings, as we have done through drugs and alcohol, we discover an alternative we never knew before. The best explanation I've ever heard for this came from a friend of mine who has been of great support to me over the past few years.

I have a really wonderful therapist who told me this not too long ago when I was completely unable to recreate my feelings about something that had happened to me: She said that pain, emotional pain, the really bad pain that comes and makes you afraid you're not going to be able to hang on, lasts between four and nine minutes; then it's gone. It might come up again, but it's just four minutes you've got to get through, or a little bit more, and then something else happens. So, my whole story about my alcoholism is what I have done to avoid those four to nine minutes.

Escape is not the route to ending the pain of addiction; it is only through having the courage to experience that pain that we can pass beyond it. These other men and women may not tell us this in their stories; nevertheless, it is possible for us to see and to hear that that is what happens *to them*. And if it happens to them, we can wonder whether the same thing will happen to us. We may find ourselves saying, "This is not at all the place I thought it was going to be! The other alcoholics who have stopped drinking sound so different. They seem to have tapped into some courage they never had before. It's in their voices, even though there's no explanation for it." Others of us may say nothing because we are too frightened to speak—even to ourselves.

"HP"

It is a moving experience to sit in a group of gay men and lesbians and hear them share honestly with one another their pain and suffering. In what others share, many of us may begin to feel a power that exceeds any individual's strength or courage. Some identify this power with the group itself. For others, the power they feel is "HP"— Higher Power. And for still others, who choose to call it God, the experience of a power greater than themselves helping them into recovery is a reconnection with a positive force in their own past from which they had isolated themselves.

Observing the changes that begin to happen in others like ourselves makes it possible for us to begin to believe it can happen to us. That we are *not* excluded from a connection with a Higher Power, with God, is a major breakthrough for most gay men and lesbians.

Homosexuals have been disowned and blacklisted by the doctrines of the major religions of the world. Because of this, many gay men and lesbians have lived feeling cut off from God for most of their lives. Cast out, scorned and rejected by the very ministers who could have helped us remain close to the support of a loving, caring source of strength and inspiration, many of us have lost faith in a Higher Power. In recovery, we discover that we no longer have to suffer this deprivation. Through *our* availability, we discover it is possible to connect with a power greater than ourselves. For many of us, this takes time. Gradually, through the painstaking process of recovery, we begin to believe in this power because we see it acting on the lives of others, as well as on our own lives. Power in action is very convincing.

Unlike straight alcoholics, gay and lesbian alcoholics have to pass through *both* edges of denial—addiction and homosexuality. For this reason, it takes many of us longer to take the second Step: "Came to believe that a power greater than ourselves could restore us to sanity." We come to believe in the help that is available to us to recover as we come to believe in ourselves as worthy of recovering. Our development of self-esteem as gay men, as lesbians, is therefore directly related to recovery from alcoholism. "Until there is somebody home, Higher Power can't get in!"

Valuing ourselves enough to answer honestly the questions about the role that alcohol plays in our lives, we embarked on Step One. Coming to believe we don't have to face the consequences alone—that there is help for us—gets us started on the second Step. By allowing ourselves to take it, we can reverse the direction of that elevator ride to the bottom of the universe and move upward toward creating a new connection with the human race. Just as we were killing ourselves with alcohol and drugs in our descent into addiction, so we are able, through believing in a Power greater than ourselves, to find our way back into life in recovery.

Carl Jung wrote about the importance of spirituality to recovery in a letter to Bill Wilson, the co-founder of Alcoholics Anonymous:

You see, "alcohol" in Latin is *spiritus*, and you use the same word for the highest religious experience as well as for the most depraving poison. The helpful formula therefore is: *spiritus contra spiritum.**

Jung's insight provides us with a life-restoring prescription: treat alcoholism with spirituality. Through sharing our experience of addiction with others who are just like ourselves, we are able to develop the spiritual connection that is central to our recovery from the disease. For many, this seems a paradox!

Paradoxes

We encounter many paradoxes on the journey into recovery. It was only when I came close to losing my life that I became willing to consider the prospect of living differently. The same is true for countless others with whom I've spoken over these years. Identifying more of these paradoxes provides additional insight:

- We find ourselves *not* alone when we thought we were most alone.
- Becoming as vulnerable as children makes it possible for us to receive the courage and strength it takes to enter recovery.
- Not by escaping but by living through the pain, we find the way to end it.
- In the stories of others' madness we are able to discover sanity for ourselves.
- Help comes when we are no longer helpless.
- This wilderness in which we find ourselves from time to time on our journey is not the *end* of the world but the *beginning* of a new one!

At the heart of all the Twelve-Step programs are the paradoxes, like "Surrender to win!" "You've got to give it away in order to keep it!" And there are many others. For me, it seems no accident that these figure so prominently in the process of recovery. Change is a terrifying process for everyone, and in order to embark on it, one

---

*This is an excerpt from a letter from Jung to Wilson, dated January 23, 1961. It was first published in the *Grapevine*, January 1963.

must reach a state of willingness. The paradox of death in life is well known to alcoholics; and the despair of those who contemplate suicide as a way out of their anguish is an experience many homosexuals can identify with. Paradox provides a synthesis of irreconcilable extremes and creates a paradigm, a model in words, for realizing something that appears to be impossible.

For many gay and lesbian addicts, recovery often seems impossible. Perhaps a major reason for this sense of hopelessness and despair is the apparent invincibility of addiction. Recovery is, itself, a paradox because it is more easily seen in others than in ourselves. Moreover, the moment they use alcohol or drugs again, alcoholics notice that the disease has advanced far beyond where they left off. The disease is in remission only as long as the addict does not use. There is no escape from this. The paradoxes help us to remember that we are only one drink away from the man, from the woman, who drank.

It takes great courage to face this. Where does this courage come from? It comes from recovery itself, in which, over and over again, we hear the words in the message both the newcomer and the old-timer bring us: "*We can do it!*" As we begin to believe this, we understand that it is only our addiction and our victim attitudes that tell us we can't.

GUIDES TO PROGRESS

No matter how she tried, Norma could not relate to the idea of a Higher Power. It might be fine for other people, but as far as she was concerned, she had gotten clear of all the male God stuff long ago and was not going to get back into that nonsense again. If it hadn't been for Nick, a biker who traveled everywhere in leather, she might have gone back out again. "Ya know, there's a place inside me, I don't know where it is, that I can feel comfortable—good about myself. That's Higher Power enough for me!" Norma decided that same place inside herself was all that *she* needed to come to believe in. And it worked; she was able to get on with her recovery.

Everyone thought Phil was really on his way into a whole new life. He was surrounded with people, and he always sounded good. He even looked healthy whenever he showed up at a meeting. The truth was that he was terrified something awful was going to happen to him and that this new way in sobriety wasn't going to last. He was sure that the unmanageability of his life as an addict would catch up with him sooner or later. He felt lost and frightened until he heard someone with a little more time in the program share the same experience. "When I start thinking like that, I know it's my addiction talking to me. And you know something? If I listen to that insanity, then I *am* insane! When I live in recovery, I'm not." Phil made the choice to live in recovery instead of addiction.

Suggestions for Action

Ask at least one person for a telephone number at every meeting you attend. Call the number that day or the next. Instead of isolating, connect with others when you feel good and when you don't. Building a network of clean and sober friends begins with the call you make today, so don't wait for tomorrow to do it. Whoever you dial needs your call as much as you need to call. (You can always begin by asking, "Is this a good time to call?" If it isn't convenient, call someone else. And if it is, whoever answers will be pleased that you were thoughtful enough to ask.)

REFLECTIONS

Our lives are a gift that has been restored to us. Celebrate the gift with sobriety.

TAKING AFFIRMATIVE ACTION

CONDITION: WILLFUL POWERLESSNESS

Practicing alcoholics are powerless over alcohol and other mind-altering substances. Even though they may not be conscious of this in their lives, they are not in control of their choices; alcohol is. Denial of this fact merely supports addiction. Alcoholics succumb to the need for substances that can satisfy the compulsion and provide relief. Addicts direct their energy toward whatever directly or indirectly rewards them with their drug of choice. On their own, they are caught in the trap that has been set and baited with alcohol and drugs.

ALTERNATIVE: WILLING, POSITIVE ACTION

Getting help is the beginning of positive action. By consciously turning over our will to this source of help, we surrender to the process of healing.

STEP THREE:

Made a decision to turn our will and our lives over to the care of God *as we understood God.*

What a strange and frightening threshold we cross when we exit the upside-down world of addiction and enter the wilderness of sobriety and abstinence! Accepting the fact that we are not alone in this unfamiliar place is often a surprise as well as a great relief, but the question of what we are supposed to do about this now brings on a sense of deep confusion.

Newcomers often share stories that confirm that, contrary to their deepest conviction that they are unique, they suffer from the double bind of denying both their addiction and their sexual preference (as far as the world is concerned). What's the next hurdle? In recovery, we are told that we are powerless, that our addictions have run our lives—and the evidence of this is too vivid to contradict. But are we supposed to wallow in this condition of powerlessness for the rest of our lives? What a way to live!

The Confusion of Powerlessness

Many newcomers, as well as old-timers in recovery, remain stuck in an intense conviction of their powerlessness. When we hear them speak, it seems they have merely exchanged one nay for another within their long history of denial. Their old tapes are still operating in the new wilderness. "There's nothing I can do to change my life! I'm powerless."

As protection against relapses, they hang on for dear life to the belief in their own powerlessness. An interesting variation is the conviction a few have in early recovery who refuse to look for employment. They are afraid that if they have money in their pockets, they'll buy alcohol or drugs. Without money, they feel they have no alternative except to stay clean and sober. Convincing themselves that their poverty *is* powerlessness, these alcoholics believe that staying broke will make it impossible for them to pick up their old habits again and fall back into addiction. This kind of thinking is rooted in old patterns of denial.

Just as in their addiction, in their recovery they stay stuck in asserting their own power to *refuse* to change. This refusal is solid evidence that they *do* have the power to change—if they choose to work at it. How difficult it is to turn the telescope around and see ourselves and the world through the other end! The Twelve Steps of the program provide the tools, the training, and the support for this. Even in early recovery it is possible to appreciate their impact on our lives.

If it were true that alcoholics had lost all power to influence or direct their lives, then none of us would have been able to attempt Step One and Step Two—"admitting we were powerless over alcohol—that our lives had become unmanageable," and "coming to believe that a Power greater than ourselves could restore us to sanity." We need the assistance of our will in order to accomplish each of these. By directing our efforts toward taking these Steps, we demonstrate that we have *not* lost the ability to change our lives.

Acknowledging we can recover is crucial to our recovery. When we do this, we assume again the responsibility we had surrendered as alcoholics. We realize that we no longer have to live at the mercy of our addiction. Accepting that we are responsible for creating a new and sober life for ourselves is often terrifying. "If I *do* have a choice whether or not I will pick up a drink, once I begin the process of recovery, then I *also* have the responsibility of making that choice!" Choice goes hand in hand with responsibility.

Victims

When we entered the wilderness of recovery, we were able to recognize in ourselves something very similar to our previous experience in addiction. It prevented us from being totally disoriented. In both settings we recognized ourselves as *victims*.

A better understanding of victims can help us link the addict with the person in recovery. We are all experts on ourselves, and one thing our expertise appreciates is our ability to suffer. Addicts are experts on suffering; we did it brilliantly and often. The shame and disgrace we endured provided us with a huge source and supply of worthlessness. For any and all reasons under the sun, we were martyrs to everything and everyone that had harmed us. As martyrs, we deserved our punishment—we were worthy of our suffering.

As victims, we were able to live in and have some sense of control over our world. This is "victim power." Whatever harm came to us (and the list of harms is endless), we could always look at it as proof of how deserving we were—as the stripes of our punishment. These fell on us from all sides, and we could suffer with an earnest conviction of our worthiness to receive them.

In early recovery, a therapist pointed out to me that every alcoholic is addicted to suffering. I was incensed at such a possibility and immediately retreated into the security of my own self-righteous denial. The suggestion that I might for one instant have gained pleasure from my suffering seemed too ludicrous for me to accept. Underneath, however, I knew it was the truth, and it forced me to examine my life as a victim in control of each misfortune and unhappiness that knocked on my door.

It became clear that whether the problem was my health, my work, or my family, I was always ready with the response, "See, what else would you expect to happen to someone like me?" Or, if something good happened, it could only be a mistake or an accident, and I dismissed it easily or turned it around to use in a negative way. This condition of willful powerlessness is immensely difficult to give up, for it proves us right in a world in which we're always wrong. None of us knows what will happen when we deprive ourselves of this power to explain our lives as victims who deserve their suffering. When we give up our victimhood, what will become of us? We face the unknown.

The recognition in sobriety that we can change this condition, that it is our choice to get help and our responsibility to use it, brings us to the edge of taking the third step of the journey into recovery. Though we are experts on suffering, we are novices about using our energy in a positive way. We have no experience with this, and it is a terrible burden, an obstacle that sets itself across our path. In the past, what have we done with obstacles like this one? That's simple. We drank or used. But now, without the alcohol or drugs that got us through difficulties like these, many of us feel lost or even helpless. This sense of helplessness causes intense confusion in recovery: we identify helplessness with powerlessness and see no way to safety except to turn back.

For gay men and lesbians, the temptation is even greater to turn back from what appears to be utter chaos in which there are no supports. Without a safety net of any kind—no alcohol or drugs— the high-wire act we have practiced during our lifetime seems impossible. We cannot take the next step; for many, this effort constitutes the turning point.

Our Old Ideas

Of all the things we must give up, our old ideas are the hardest. For years, these old ideas have flourished in our garden. They have become planted so firmly that they have taken over. To some of us, it may even appear that these weeds are all that grow there now. The process of recovery is one of gradually rooting out ideas that are no longer of any help or use. This process makes room for new ideas that bring new life and growth again into the garden. We can begin by acknowledging that the weather, "the climate" of our minds, may not always be favorable for such efforts. We cannot delay doing this if we are to make our way forward beyond this place.

Working honestly and consistently at taking Step One and Step Two has already had an impact upon us. We have identified the problem that exists in our physical and mental life as alcoholics: the unmanageability and insanity of addiction. Because Step Three identifies the problem that exists in our spiritual life, it is no wonder that we balk at it!

For a complex variety of reasons related to the way in which we grew up and were loved or not loved, some of us may have thought of ourselves as emotionally handicapped. In this predicament, our inadequacies and helplessness got certain kinds of responses from others that removed the necessity for us to be responsible for ourselves. Many people in recovery know that these emotional handicaps are serious, but when it comes to *spiritual* helplessness, most of us feel completely lost in the wilderness. This is much more than we bargained for!

Many gay men and lesbians have grown up in Western religions in which bigotry and hypocrisy about their sexual orientation have flourished. Because of this, they were prevented from developing and evolving a healthy spiritual center in their lives. Scorned, shunned, and punished for their homosexuality, some have turned their backs on any possibility of spiritual comfort and support.

What words does a lesbian use who has never felt she could pray to a God from either the Old *or* the New Testament? What prayer does a gay man say who has been abandoned by his family and his church?

To compensate for this spiritual deprivation and hardship, gay people sometimes affirm themselves in a very different way. "If God doesn't want to have anything to do with us, then we don't want to have anything to do with God! We don't need God, spirituality, or anything like that in our lives, and we refuse to invoke the name in prayer in any and all things. We're fine, on our own, just the way we are, thank you. And we don't need anyone who thinks we're not!" Others choose silence.

In recovery, as we continue the journey, we need to let go of this idea. Instead of isolating ourselves, we have to learn to participate in the process. As difficult as it may be, gay men and lesbians need to prepare to make themselves available in a way that may be new. To do this, we have to allow both time and space within us for a power greater than ourselves to show up.

Popular culture communicates deep philosophical truths in many ingenious ways. One of the least tedious is the bumper sticker. Two of these gems seem apt here: Please Don't Walk on the Water, and the simple acknowledgment, Not God! Each one suggests how we may understand what needs to be done in order to take the third Step. The spiritual dimension of our lives, which was taken over by addiction to substances, has been fertile ground for the disease. By relinquishing our own claim to filling this dimension, we become available to a power greater than ourselves to do this for us. The recognition that we need to get out of the way in order to accomplish this is essential for recovery.

Such a recognition does not happen overnight; deprivation is not a condition corrected with one or even two meals. It may take days or months or years of Twelve-Step meetings for us to begin to allow the nourishment of the spiritual food that others share to enter our lives. Many recovering people experience a "spiritual awakening" during the third year, or later. This takes as long as it takes. Remember the long distance we travel just to find our way into the meeting rooms. Gaining sustenance from what is said there requires time and patience.

The disease of alcoholism *is* cunning and baffling; addiction is pernicious. We need to constantly remember that the power restored to us in early recovery can once again be diverted into the loop of our addiction. This is a crucial reason for surrendering it to a power greater than ourselves who can provide us with good, orderly direction. It should come as no surprise that the old familiar willfulness is always ready and waiting to yield to old habits. Turning this will over to a Higher Power offers insurance against slipping back into addiction again.

Perfectionism

Another old idea of gigantic proportion in the lives of many gay men and lesbians is the unattainable goal of perfection. Using it to stand as the opposite limit from the zero of victimhood, we filled the void in between. This notion is deeply ingrained in every alcoholic, gay or straight. For the gay man and lesbian, however, being the best has often meant choosing different kinds of goals from straight men and women. Some gay men have considered certain avenues of expression or competition closed to them. They have devoted a great deal of time and energy to the pursuit of appetite gratification. The stories they share about their sexual exploits are clearly demonstrations of "besting" any other male around.

Many other gay men and lesbians, to prove themselves outstanding professionals, become workaholics and devote incredible amounts of energy and time to being the best in their jobs and hobbies. This experience shared with me by Arthur is very common for alcoholics, co-alcoholics, and co-dependents:

From his college days into his career as an architect, Arthur prepared for examinations, conferences and presentations, for everything, in a way that went far beyond what was necessary or helpful. He was always ready for a siege even though he might be just going on a reconnaisance mission. He used alcohol more and more to make life bearable, until after a long sequence of blackouts he was almost killed by a seizure.

In recovery, we discover there is a middle range between the best or the worst. In the middle range, we discover opportunities to develop different kinds of lives. We no longer need to swing from being victim to victor, from being damaged goods to heroic gods and goddesses. We begin to develop our personhood and stop trying to walk on the water, and we learn what it is like to give up playing God.

The pedestal of perfectionism stands in the way of discovering the middle range. This pedestal needs dismantling. Sometimes it is only one brick at a time. Attending Twelve-Step meetings is vital to the process, because in them we can learn how other people are working on this task. From insights we get from others about what they are doing, we can begin to understand how we can get our own obstacles out of our way. Their sharing removes the bricks from their path, and when we get up enough courage to tell our own stories, we discover a tiny bit more room in which we can also move forward.

Developing a Spiritual Center in Recovery

Sharing our experience clears away space for recovery. Gradually, we develop a spiritual sensitivity that is different from the religion-centered training we had from any church or any clergyman in our entire lives. It is a phenomenon many have known, even those who are most negative about religion, prayer, or a Higher Power. The gradual development of a spiritual dimension in our lives begins with sharing our experience, strength and hope with others who do the same with us. When we clear away the cluttered shambles of our past, the space we create begins to be permeated with a new spiritual vitality. The development of a spiritual center within us is the result of this new energy operating in our lives.

Healing is an unusually difficult phenomenon to describe. There is something inexplicable, miraculous, about it. Some individuals who have suffered the greatest physical, emotional and mental ravages, contrary to all expectation, have made unbelievable progress in recovering from the effects of alcohol and drugs. Others, with apparently much less damage to their systems, have succumbed to organ malfunction and the complications of heart, liver, or other diseases. Physicians with whom I have spoken confess their inability to account for some of these amazing results, and though scientific evidence can provide data, it does not answer the deepest questions about why one person recovers and another succumbs.

It is not the need of the individual but the *wish* of the individual that counts. There is an often-quoted slogan that captures this idea: "AA is not for those who need it but for those who want it." This applies, as well, to the families, lovers and friends of alcoholics. How difficult it is for them to accept that it is not *their* wish that counts! It must be the one who suffers from the disease who wants to begin recovery. We must want it for ourselves or else the attempt will be short-lived, doomed to failure from the start. We may enter recovery for many reasons; however, until we want it for *ourselves*, it will not happen for us.

But, once again, the familiar paradox appears. Even though it is the will, the wish, that must operate, we must get out of our own way in order to allow the recovery process to proceed. When addicts refuse to turn over the process of recovery to a Higher Power, or to have faith in a power beyond themselves—such as the group, or the Twelve-Step program—and insist on running the show, they discover they are back again in the driver's seat. In addicted bodies and minds, they are driving without any understanding of the terrain in which they find themselves or the vehicle they drive. Isolated from the healing forces that flow to them through others, they are on a collision course with addiction again.

Alcoholics have lived close to danger knowingly and unknowingly during active addiction. We have risked our position, our health, our very existence just to go on using alcohol and drugs. Addicts are accustomed to taking extravagant risks—living dangerously. In the dysfunctional homes we grew up in as children, ominous situations were not at all uncommon. As adults, many of us continued to confuse danger with sex, love or intimacy. It is ironic that in early recovery we feel such enormous fear at taking risks. It has been suggested that when we are under the illusion that we're in control, we love living on the edge—with all its anxiety. Without that illusion, we balk at the brink.

The basic rules for the child growing up in a dysfunctional family are these: Don't Trust; Don't Feel; and Don't Talk.* Taking Step

---

*Claudia Black, *It Will Never Happen to Me!* (Denver: M.A.C. Printing and Publications Division, 1982), 31–49.

Three is therefore the most difficult of all in early recovery. Those three rules are reason why so many back off. Without any faith or belief in anyone except ourselves, it seems impossible to turn over our will to a Higher Power who is still remote and strange. It feels exactly like stepping off solid ground into nothingness and expecting to be supported by something that might not be there.

However, many recovering gay men and lesbians have found a way to take this Step even though they considered themselves unbelievers or outcasts from any and all religions. They took Step Three by acting "as-if" they believed they would be helped. They allowed themselves the same benefit as those who did believe in the healing ability of a power greater than themselves to assist them in their recovery. They made a leap into as-if, they allowed their unbelief not to get in their way!

Help Is Available to Us

The Steps, the meetings, and the literature that is available in the rooms before and after people share their stories provide us with the source of help we need to begin the journey. An additional source is the idea of sponsorship that the Twelve-Step programs have developed. It is one of the most valuable tools offered to the recovering alcoholic.

Going to meetings, working the Steps, and reading the literature makes us available to the program recommendation that we find a sponsor to help us apply these tools in our daily lives. By the time we reach Step Three, we should follow through on that recommendation. This is a big decision for many of us; nevertheless, choosing a sponsor is part of a program of recovery.

Let's consider why. A sponsor is someone who has gone through the hell of addiction and the hardship of entering and making progress in recovery. Enlisting the support of a person just like ourselves, we leave our isolation behind and acknowledge hope, as well as help, from this individual whose sobriety we admire and wish for ourselves. The person we choose to help us find our way on our journey is someone with whom it is possible to form an intimate human connection with life beyond addiction. As alcoholics, we need to learn how to do this. We would not be where we are now if we had learned this before.

Straight men and women in recovery are encouraged to choose sponsors of the same sex. For a gay man or a lesbian, it is often a good idea to ask someone of the opposite sex to be a sponsor. Sponsors are chosen not for romance but for sobriety! If you have unresolved sexual or other kinds of issues, it is helpful to choose a sponsor who can help you to focus on sobriety in early recovery instead of fanning these other issues into flame.

One good way to discover how well you work together is to ask someone to be a temporary sponsor. Set a time limit of one to three months in which to find out if you get the support and direction you need in the way that you need it. Either you or the sponsor can identify reasons for going on together or choosing a new temporary sponsor at the end of this period. Sponsorship is always a two-way street. It must work for the sponsor as well as the sponsee.

Remember that sponsors are not for life; we can change them when we choose. We may also have several at the same time, depending on our needs. Choosing and working with a sponsor is one of the key positive actions we can take to support recovery. Review this brief checklist in considering people you might ask to be a sponsor.

Do these individuals have:
- sufficient length of time in AA, along with a solid understanding and commitment to Twelve-Step programs?
- a positive attitude toward recovery in themselves and other people?
- an honest way of sharing the details of their own addiction and the work they are doing on themselves in recovery?
- openmindedness in handling problems and considering alternatives?
- the time and availability to work with you?
- sound suggestions to offer that you can count on being shared with you?
- personal characteristics that encourage your trust? (In addition to age, sex, etc., these include respect for anonymity and confidentiality.)

- the tough-mindedness to call you on old ways of thinking and acting?
- the kind of self-esteem that encourages your own self-esteem?
- the kind of sobriety you want?

If you have not found a sponsor by the time you begin to work on Step Three, it is vitally important to (1) set yourself the priority of getting a sponsor (or a temporary sponsor); (2) approach people you'd like to ask, and discuss it with them; and (3) accept your efforts as positive, instead of rejecting yourself when others decline your request. It's not by burying our head in powerlessness but by taking affirmative action that we progress on the journey. Whether we find it easy or difficult to accept the idea of turning our will and our lives over to the care of a Higher Power, we can use the sponsor to extend the entire opportunity of recovery for ourselves. Having a sponsor who is knowledgeable about working the Steps and who is willing to work with us is like having the AA Big Book on-line. We make it much easier on ourselves when we use the tools of the program.

Another tool of the program is a prayer that has sustained many on their journey in time of crisis as well as in repose. It is often recited at the beginning or the end of meetings, and the first two verses are familiar to many hundreds of thousands of people in recovery. The entire prayer, which has been attributed to Reinhold Niebuhr, may be of special help to those of us who already experience a connection with a spiritual force and who wish to call upon this power to assist our recovery.

The Serenity Prayer

God grant me the
Serenity to accept the things
I cannot change;

Courage to change the things I
can; and
Wisdom to know the difference.

Living one day at a time;
Enjoying one moment at a time;
Accepting hardship
As the pathway to peace;

Taking, as God did, this
world as it is, not as I would
have it;

Trusting that God will make all
things right if I surrender
to God's will;

That I may be reasonably happy
in this life, and supremely
happy with God forever in
the next.
Amen.

When we step beyond the threshold on Step Three, we initiate the affirmative action that is necessary at this moment in our journey into recovery.

GUIDES TO PROGRESS

Jeff couldn't stand being told that he had to do *anything*! He hated when his parents had done it, and now that he was on his own, he certainly wasn't going to let anyone else do it to him. He was the boss! His DWI's had gotten him into a program for drunk drivers, but that would soon be over and life could go back to normal—except that people were telling him he had to stop drinking or something really bad would happen to him. How did they know? It was true that his life was going better since he had quit using, and he wasn't going to lose his job as he had thought several weeks ago. What was all this noise about "Turn it over!" he kept hearing? As long as he did it, he had to admit that everything had turned around for him. So that's what he did, a day at a time.

During her whole life, Mollie felt that she had been bullied—by her father, her brothers, men in general. She avoided them and surrounded herself with a close circle of lesbian friends with whom she went to the bars and drank. The day her roommate, Nan, took her to a Twelve-Step meeting, she had an instant aversion to Step Three and decided that if that's what it took for her to begin recovery, she couldn't handle it. At a women's meeting Nan then persuaded her to attend, Mollie heard another lesbian share her thoughts about turning her will and her life over to a Higher Power who wasn't male. That, Mollie admitted, was something she could think about. She made this meeting her home group, where she soon became coffee maker and, in time, secretary.

Suggestions for Action

After observing your perfectionism in action, ask yourself whether you might be able to get along without it. Are you willing to attempt this? If you are, allow yourself for ten minutes or half an hour at a time the luxury of accepting things and people *exactly as they are* without changing them. Then, perhaps, try it for an hour or two, and then an afternoon or an evening here and there. We get valuable feedback when we check with ourselves how much lighter it feels to live without perfectionism. It is possible, however, that the loss of such a weight may be too unsettling and require considerable attention and monitoring.

REFLECTIONS

We come a long way toward finding our courage and experiencing our serenity when we support ourselves with the wisdom we have developed in our lives.

Step Four

LOOKING INTO THE MIRROR

CONDITION: SELF-DELUSION

Escaping into fantasy, for many of us, was the only way we knew to stay sane. We deluded ourselves that our lives worked, and that nothing was wrong with us a few drinks couldn't improve. "Everyone has problems," we told ourselves. Our solution to all those problems, in time, was alcohol or drugs. A crisis—health, employment, financial, relationship, or legal—forced us to see that our lives were falling apart not because of the problems but because of our solution. We had been sent down the road to total destruction by dishonesty and self-delusion.

ALTERNATIVE: SELF-REVELATION

Looking at what is, instead of what isn't, testing the reality of the experience of our life as gay men, as lesbians, is essential for recovery. At Twelve-Step meetings and one-on-one, we learn that our "awful-terribles" are not so awful or terrible when someone else speaks them. When we look into the mirror of the meeting, we see ourselves!

STEP FOUR:

Made a searching and fearless moral inventory of ourselves.

Our thinking processes are carefully evolved and developed over the years of our lives. The influence of alcohol or drugs on how we think is not ended forever just because we stop using them. The way I think about myself and about the world today is deeply affected by what I have experienced as an alcoholic, and I believe, the same is true for others in recovery.

Masks and Criticism

Most gay men and lesbians have grown up and lived under conditions that inhibit healthy mental and emotional development. The experience of lying to others, wearing masks—removing one, putting on another, whenever the occasion calls for it (and sometimes even when the occasion doesn't)—is very familiar. Mask-changing is a habit that becomes so natural we rarely acknowledge we are doing it. Having grown up in straight households, we have developed a common sense understanding of what it takes to go incognito among the people who care about us as well as those who don't. We do what we think will work for as long as we think necessary. In the presence of others, we are performers. When we stand alone in front of the mirror, we are critics of ourselves.

Gay men and lesbians, as a group, may be the largest "critical mass" in society. The expertise derived from self-criticism has honed this ability so sharp that it functions with little or no restraint under any and all circumstances. For some, being hypercritical is a source of humor and delight. For others, it is the cause of deep dissatisfaction with family, friends, and strangers, as well as the basis of their own depression; the critical voices inside their own heads never stop for a moment.

How else is it possible to be "the best little girl" or "the best little boy" in the house, the neighborhood, the school, the town, the *world*? Unless one works at self-criticism every waking hour, this goal of imagined perfection is unattainable. This perfectionistic kind of thinking, on both the conscious and the unconscious level, is vivid and familiar to gay people. Alcoholics drink over it constantly.

Gay men and lesbians have particular difficulty looking at their own hypercritical attitudes and self-contempt and activating the "pause" button on this way of thinking. The distorted rules of survival we have learned have made us feel less acceptable as human beings. This mode of thinking has often become so natural that the suggestion that it should be examined meets with powerful resistance. For gay people, showing up in life—participating completely—has always meant either being criticized or else criticizing everything and everybody, especially themselves.

Using alcohol or drugs is at first the only means many of us know for anesthetizing the pain we feel over not being perfect. Some of us translate not being perfect into meaning that we are not lovable. Alcohol and drugs can deaden the pain of feeling unloved and the suffering that comes from having a poor self-concept, a self-image distorted by internalized homophobia, and low self-esteem. Escaping into fantasy and self-delusion is a welcome relief from the barrage of criticism that continually eats away at us. For a period of time, the silence we achieve with drugs and alcohol even sounds like sanity—until the madness of addiction takes over.

With drugs and alcohol, however, we add even more strident voices to the chorus of self-destruction. Our self-criticism intensifies, as does the criticism we get from others. What appeared to be escape turns into a head-on collision with unmanageability.

Addiction feeds on criticism because its message is always clear and consistent: *"You can't do anything without ME!"* Alcoholics who are still using cannot allow themselves to believe in support for handling life *without* alcohol and drugs. Recognizing the need for support from others is one of the first indications that we are getting ready to begin implementing the process of change.

It often takes a long time to reach this awareness. But even when we do, we do not immediately recast the mold in which we have trained our minds to think. If we have carefully taken the first three steps of the journey into recovery, we have achieved some new and valuable understanding about ourselves. We have been able to observe, in action, how our minds make everything far more complicated than it actually is. No matter what circumstance is presented, the addictive mind will complicate it. And if there is only silence, this same mind will create its own pandemonium to insure that the alcoholic remains a victim. It is the pattern of addictive thinking to generate suffering. We generate our secrets out of this same pattern.

Our Secrets

During Hal's earliest days of coming to Twelve-Step meetings, one of the first slogans he learned was, "We are only as sick as our secrets." With that reminder alone, he knew he was *very* sick because of the thousands of secrets he lived with. There was no area of his life without secrets. A shocking realization came to him as he sat listening while others shared their stories: these people were telling intimate details about themselves he never believed could be told! For him, this was the beginning of understanding what change would be like in his life. For him to be able to do what those people were doing, he knew he would have to change. At that time, he didn't know how, or if he even wanted to.

When he shared this in the meeting, he was reminded that everyone in the room had been just like him when they started. The only reason they were doing what they did was because they each truly wanted to recover from addiction. If that was what he wanted, then he'd just have to find the way to dump all of his "precious" secrets. Hal had never thought of them as "precious," and it certainly startled him when they were referred to like that.

The truth has an unusual way of reaching into our lives. Indeed, our secrets are precious to us whether or not they are to anybody else. For me, there was one secret that outweighed all the rest—and it was the one that caused me the greatest suffering: I was gay and afraid someone would find out. Damn right that was a "precious" secret! Damn right I had to suffer over it! That, at least, is what I thought back in the beginning of my recovery.

During the past eight years, many gay men and lesbians have told me how difficult recovery was for them as long as they kept their homosexuality a secret. The deep-seated fear of discovery, of not being accepted, of being thrown out of the meeting, continues to inhibit gay people from sharing major problems they are facing. At the least, it motivates them to change gender pronouns when referring to loved ones. In each of the Twelve-Step programs, except in gay meetings, hiding or lying about sexual orientation is more common than honestly revealing it to others.

In spite of the insistence that all alcoholics are alike, at straight meetings most gay men and lesbians experience a deep sense of uniqueness, a feeling they are different from everyone else. Denying the validity of the experience of being gay in the midst of a hetero-sexist society harms us further. Many of us have endured this painful confrontation between our new truth-telling and our still-existent se-crets. But that is precisely what the gay men and lesbians I've spoken to have done: *endured* it by hiding behind old masks or by lying.

Using what happens (or doesn't happen) at a meeting as the reason for picking up a drink again is more self-delusion. There are all kinds of meetings. We have to find the ones in which we get the support we need for our recovery—whether it is in straight meetings or gay meetings. It is up to us to discover where to find support.

Those of us who find our way into gay meetings are fortunate because we can more easily let go of the secrets that have often led to relapse for gay and lesbian addicts. In places where gay meetings are not available, sharing these secrets with a gay sponsor is very helpful. Sponsors need not live in the same town or state; there is always a telephone handy to call them. When sobriety comes first, letting go of the burden of our secrets will definitely improve our chances of not picking up the first drink or drug again.

"Who Wants to Know?"

Relapse is common, and the causes of relapse are the habits we have formed in addiction, as well as in childhood. These habits do not fall away from us easily. We program our minds with these pat-terns of thinking. Holding on to our deepest, darkest secrets about our sexuality has been a way of life for us. The prospect of living without this secret is beyond anything most of us have ever hoped, and the suggestion that we share the truth about ourselves with some-one else causes tremendous anxiety. What would it be like to live *without* our secret?

That answer waits behind another question: Who wants to know? When we stop using alcohol and drugs, everything around us changes. If *we* do not change, we will resume using alcohol or drugs again to endure what we perceive to be the intolerable experience of living. But if we wish to recover, if we choose to live in sobriety, we have the choice of coming forward with the answer to that question. We need to want recovery enough, however, in order to speak out with a voice that affirms this wish.

None of the Twelve-Step programs are for gay people who need them; they are for gay people who *want* them. As soon as we become clear about that, we begin to understand in a very practical way how the programs work. They work because we work at them. Very slowly, through the efforts we make, the programs begin to work in us. Our patterns of thinking are modified gradually by the effect of the process of recovery in our lives. Our actions reflect the changes. Even though the compulsion to drink or to use may not have left us, we do not act on it because we have worked at altering our old way of thinking not with drugs or alcohol but with sane and sober ideas. These new and different ideas we have struggled to implement are the simplified form of the first three Steps of the Twelve-Step programs:

"I can't. God/HP (Higher Power) can. Let God/HP."

They are the first steps of our ascent out of the darkness of addiction. Now, with one foot already on the fourth step, it is essential we reassure ourselves that the way forward is by taking it.

Making Our List

We begin by looking at ourselves not for the old, familiar purpose of suffering and self-destruction but for a positive reason: our continued progress depends on honesty. Instead of hiding behind masks, we need to look at ourselves and acknowledge what we see.

To some, this suggestion may seem like an invitation to create a catalogue of disasters. In recovery, however, there is no need for any bills of indictment. Step Four is an inventory that identifies our positive aspects—our assets—as well as areas for improvement. Unless we include both, the list is worthless. We have made a habit of deluding ourselves about the good things as well as the less good. We need to bear this in mind. The mere fact that any of us have survived long enough to begin the process of recovery is sufficient evidence of strengths. These strengths, like courage and determination, absolutely belong on the plus side of the ledger.

It is not by burying our misconceptions and distortions under more lies but by revealing them to ourselves in an honest and conscientious manner that we continue our progress in recovery. Our secrets will continue to keep us sick unless we get rid of them! Our health depends on our willingness to undertake this effort at self-disclosure.

Most of us strongly resist writing this inventory. Our resistance is closely linked with the habit of denial and is intimately related to our dependence on self-delusion. Confronting this self-delusion is the only way through it.

With this Step, we the have unusual opportunity to see ourselves as no longer being the frightened and confused children who were forced to make up our own unique rules. Remember those rules we created in order to survive:

> Be perfect!
> Be a rescuer!
> Be silent and unnoticed!
> Be funny!
> Don't look like a queer!

Those rules got us through childhood in our dysfunctional families and in the schools and neighborhoods we lived in. Unless we are willing to look at ourselves, at who we are now and how we do things now, we will continue to act as if we were still children. We can make honest and meaningful choices about how we wish to be and act during the rest our lives only *after* we have seen ourselves the way we are and the way we have been. The journey out of self-delusion is through self-revelation.

For years, we have lived in an arena jammed with criticism of ourselves and all the things we have done, as well as the way we have done them; about how our gay orientation has been the cause of so much suffering and unhappiness to others; about how badly we have mistreated others; about how justly we deserve the punishment—the disgrace—that has been meted out to us, and so on. Each of us has our own code words to unlock the door to suffering and guilt over the past. It's magic how well they work! We carried with us the burden of criticism—our own and others,—wherever we went, even though we pretended we were leaving it behind. We escaped into fantasy, and, in our fantasy, we found our way into addiction as our bodies became chemically dependent.

Thirty years ago I heard an ancient story about a weary Chinese traveler on the road to a city he had never visited before. He had journeyed a long distance and lost his way many times. Finally, he saw a man sitting on a fence beside the road and his burden of discouragement seemed to melt into the air. "Please, sir, can you tell me how far it is to the city of Chang An?" he asked the man. With the utmost seriousness, the man answered, "It is only six miles, sir, but it is better not to start from here."

This is the place that we *must* start from, because this is where we find ourselves now in our journey into recovery: facing the unfaceable. Our secrets form an integral part of the way we think about others and ourselves. Living with them as we have done over the years, we are imprisoned in the past. Many alcoholics have found out the hard way that they will drink and use again and again over these same secrets. Secrets support alcoholism and addiction; each one of them lies ready and waiting for us to say the code words that can release them into action.

To those who begin working on this inventory, some of these darkest secrets are often a great surprise. As we begin on ones we knew were there, we discover many others crawling around beneath the first rock. Pursuing the effort to develop the list further, we find ourselves able to reach far back into childhood and the secrets we buried there. One secret is tied to another, and that one to still another. Secrets we never even knew existed appear as we patiently go about developing the list.

Remember that we are not making a perfect, exhaustive list. We are merely identifying those aspects of our lives that wait in hiding and pounce on us when we are most vulnerable, when we think we have escaped from the wreckage of our past. In this list, we are also identifying the patient, courageous, loving parts of ourselves that have helped us to sustain our lives through the darkest moments. It is important to remember to write only what comes up for us now. Later on in sobriety, other secrets will reveal themselves. It is a good idea to use this Step as one of the first opportunities in sobriety *not* to be perfect.

Unfortunately, many alcoholics make this task an obstacle instead of looking at it as the action required to overcome the roadblocks standing in the way of recovery. They work through the first three Steps and then avoid Steps Four and Five. It is only later, when they are baffled and cannot understand why they have difficulty making major strides forward that they discover the reason is quite simple.

Their secrets sentence them to live under conditions similar to those they knew in addiction.

Discovering ourselves as gay men and lesbians—what we are like, what we have done, what we have not done, what our assets and liabilities are—is astounding. Developing this inventory is the first time that many of us move out from behind the shadow of criticism of ourselves. Our thoughts about ourselves and our actions have actually been the source for much negativity in our lives, and it is possible to see and understand this as we go through the process of developing the list of secrets.

What others have shared in meetings may provide us with support and encouragement when we write an inventory. Indeed, many of us discovered only after we had begun writing how much we had in common with other gay and lesbian alcoholics. But someone else's secrets do not keep us locked in the past; only *our own* prevent us really from being available to change our lives for the future.

The perspective we create through making the inventory separates us from those obstacles. This is extremely valuable for our recovery. We can encourage this perspective by observing three things:

(1) ourselves as the source and support of the obstacles;
(2) the obstacles themselves that we have created and supported; and
(3) that we are capable of standing apart from both our support for the obstacles and the obstacles themselves.

When we do this, we can begin to appreciate our potential for living a new and different life in sobriety. We discover that we no longer have to choose to be the same obstacle-maker, nor continue to hold on to those obstacles that are standing in the way of our recovery.

In addiction, we have lived as if we were caught, and our minds became accustomed to this manner of thinking. That is why it is so important in early sobriety to experience the possibility of a different perspective, one that is free of this feeling of victimization. Through developing the inventory, we create the opportunity for changing the way we think by revealing ourselves to ourselves from the perspective of this moment, now. The fear of looking at ourselves in the present as objectively as possible has kept many of us stuck in the bottle. We have allowed fear to control our lives through our secrets from the past. This Step offers us the chance to move beyond this addictive way of thinking into the present.

Developing an Inventory

Each day, when we look in the mirror, we see what we choose to see. At any moment, we may have an "attack of the uglies" and see ourselves as ugly. When this passes, we see different things about ourselves. The truth is that there are certain features we like about ourselves and others we don't. Observing what is there *within* ourselves, as honestly as we are able, and allowing ourselves to create a list of what we see, is the task we undertake in the fourth Step.

There is extensive guidance available for developing our inventories.* The following suggestions may also be helpful for gay men and lesbians who choose any of the available guides. These are merely suggestions; consider them carefully before following through on them.

- Discuss your intention to write a Fourth Step inventory with your sponsor.
- Develop an outline that will cover the areas you most need to focus on. (The general fourth Step guides may be exactly what you need. You may also find you need greater depth in areas you find deeply troubling, such as your childhood, violence, incest, internalized homophobia, or health issues.)
- Set a period of time in which you will complete the inventory, and develop a plan to accomplish it. Set aside time to write, and make it a priority in your schedule.
- Use your own words instead of language that may sound "better" after you edit it. (Your own words have special meaning for you, and it is important to connect this with your feelings.)

---

*See, for example, *Alcoholics Anonymous* (New York: Alcoholics Anonymous World Services, Inc., 1976), 64–71; and *The Twelve Steps of Alcoholics Anonymous*, interpreted by the Hazelden Foundation (San Francisco: Harper & Row, 1987), 28–58.

- Write whatever comes up for you, and then go on to the next thing; don't get stuck in any one area.
- Stay in close touch with others via telephone and meetings; don't get out on a limb all by yourself just because you're writing your inventory.
- Share your experience—what it's like for you—with others one-on-one and in meetings; you will support others who are doing a fourth Step and, at the same time, receive support for yourself.
- Don't minimize your efforts or your feelings. This is a unique opportunity for you to see yourself as you are.
- Allow others to support and love you in your process of getting better. No matter what you discover about yourself, you are taking the action that is needed to change.
- Keep in mind that Step Four is a vital part of the process of helping you feel better—not worse—about yourself. It is a step toward recovery and not backward into addiction.

We need to identify our strengths along with the areas for improvement in our lives. Listing "faults" or "defects of character" can easily pander to the victim in us who cannot get enough of suffering. Several decades ago, when they wrote some of the guidance material, the founders of the AA program used language that was appropriate to their time. Today, instead of *faults, defects of character, shortcomings*, we know that a phrase like *survival tactics* is often closer to the mark when it comes to revealing what we did to get through our lives.

The guidance and support of a sponsor can be invaluable for anyone engaged in writing an inventory. We need to learn to use this important tool of the program, because sponsors are a significant part of our recovery. No longer do we have to be alone. Working with a sponsor is an excellent way of developing a new model of relationship, a new framework for intimacy, that does not confuse love with sex. Gay men and lesbians need to use this opportunity to discover what a relationship with another person who cares about them can mean—without sex.

A gay or lesbian sponsor with several years of recovery in a Twelve-Step program can help us through the major ordeal of owning our homosexuality. Having made a secret of our sexual orientation all our lives, having created hundreds and even thousands of lies and secrets behind it as well, we may find the prospect of bringing it into the light too formidable for the thimbleful of sobriety we have so far been able to accumulate. Postponing the day, however, may create another delusion: that there is "an easier, softer way." We should look at the possibility that our progress in recovery can be greatly advanced if we get rid of this secret—and all the rest—instead of holding on to it. It is our alcoholic way of thinking that makes us believe otherwise.

I have never known any man or woman to write "heterosexuality" as a character defect on their fourth Step inventory. I have known many gay men and lesbians to put "homosexuality" at the top of this list. This perspective is symptomatic of a pattern of thinking that thrives on criticism. Being gay or being lesbian is as much a "defect of character" as having blue eyes when 90 percent of the population has brown eyes. When we think of the items on our list of "short-comings" as either *survival tactics* or *obstacles to recovery*, we can understand that our sexual orientation doesn't belong there. We are who we are!

Pretending to be what we are *not* is precisely what we are striving to put behind us. That some of us have basically negative thoughts about ourselves because we are homosexuals, and that we endure a tremendous amount of self-hatred over being homosexual is the truth and the end to the pretense for many of us. The truth is no delusion. Accepting this truth is as important to our progress in recovery as breathing fresh air, exercising and eating nutritious food.

Facing ourselves, acknowledging how seriously self-hatred has influenced our lives, dismantles one of our basic obstacles. All the rest of our obstacles must take second, third, fourth, fifth place behind it.

So many of us have deluded ourselves into thinking that we were born with our hypercritical attitude! When we write "homosexuality" on the inventory, we know this is a lie. And we know, at the same moment, that we have survived *in spite of* the lie. Once we discover that we have survived something that almost killed us, what should we do? In the Book of Exodus, we are told that the children of Israel sang a great song when they reached the other shore of the Red Sea. We, too, can celebrate our survival through our sobriety by continuing to develop the inventory of our secrets, our obstacles, and the strengths that supported us to get us through thus far.

Unless we can own ourselves, we are nothing. No matter what secrets we have kept about ourselves, we can write them on the page and acknowledge them. In the privacy of this sober room of our house, we can take off the mask and look at what *is* instead of continuing with the pretense of what *isn't*. As gay men, as lesbians, this is a reality-test of our lives as we have lived them. "Mirror, mirror, on the wall. . ." In the reflection of this inventory, we see who we are, and we discover we no longer have to turn away. Nor does the world implode when we become honest. Our thinking processes are encouraged to evolve in a healthier environment, one that supports recovery instead of addiction.

GUIDES TO PROGRESS

The first two weeks without alcohol or marijuana had passed, and as difficult as they had been, Greg was happy about the progress he was making in recovery. As more time passed, he began to find himself more and more irritable. He blew up several times over little things in conversation with his lover, Paul. Even though he talked about it with a friend he had come to trust in the program, he still was very critical of himself for these incidents. "I'm doing the *best* I can, and still things like this are constantly happening!" he told the friend.

"Sounds like more perfectionism to me. Why don't you stop telling yourself you're doing the best you can and say that you're doing *what* you can? That's the truth, isn't it?" Greg agreed that he always felt he could do better, no matter how well he did, and it felt a lot easier to accept that he was doing *what* he could instead. By "lightening up" on himself, he discovered that he became less and less irritable.

Gigi met Nina at the second lesbian Twelve-Step meeting she attended, and she fell head over heels in love. She couldn't understand why Nina, who had six months of sobriety, was playing so hard to get. After a few weeks, Nina went out for coffee with her. "You know, Gigi, I like you very much, and I can tell that you like me. I've got a lot to learn about myself during this first year in recovery— and so do you. That's why I've got to keep the focus on me, instead of getting involved in a relationship with anyone. Why don't we work on our recovery first before we start anything else? If something is going to happen between us, then it'll happen in sobriety." This wasn't what Gigi wanted to hear, but it made sense the more she thought about it. Sobriety was the priority; her relationship with Nina was a bonus that was waiting for her out there in recovery.

Suggestions for Action

Before you start to think about doing a fourth Step inventory, spend some time looking at honesty and what it feels like to be honest in your life. Take five to ten minutes once, or even twice, a day to listen to everything that comes out of your mouth when you speak with another person. Most of the time, we're on "automatic." It can be very revealing to discover who you are and how honest you are when you speak with others. Listen, and benefit from what you learn about yourself.

REFLECTIONS

We are loving people. We can embrace ourselves today for our efforts to be channels of love and recovery.

CATHARSIS

CONDITION: REGRESSION AND/OR STAGNATION

Life in addiction is filled with pain and suffering, but salty tears are sweet to the addict. We learn to love suffering. This pattern comes with us into recovery when we experience the terror of revealing ourselves to another human being. "If someone knows me, knows everything about me, then I can't go on doing crazy things. *I'll have to change!*" Or, "If they really knew what I was like, they wouldn't have anything to do with me!" Fear of losing what we already have, no matter how little it may be, causes us to dig in our heels. We find ourselves slipping back into our old ways.

ALTERNATIVE: CLEANSING AND RENEWAL

We end suffering by sharing our inventory of secrets with another human being. Clearing out the wreckage of the past begins with taking inventory of that wreckage, along with our strengths, and going on from there. We make a fresh start when we clean house.

STEP FIVE:

Admitted to God, to ourselves, and to another human being the exact nature of our wrongs.

Living in a maze of obstacles generated by our secrets is a test of ingenuity as well as a constant drain on our energy. We tell ourselves, "With him and her and him (but *not* him), I can be honest; with her and her and him, I can't: With *X* and *Y*, we know the score about each other and can play the game, but with the rest, no way!" It takes infinite skill to remember who knows what about whom. Now and then, we make a devastating mistake by sharing something with someone we didn't want him or her to know. Secrets complicate our lives, fragment them into a kaleidoscope of suffering and misery; and we pay a high price for keeping them.

During our active addiction, a few rare moments may surface in which we have the experience of just not giving a damn. We wish the whole labyrinth of lies would collapse. What a tremendous burden to be relieved of! But then, the thought slips away somehow, and we are back again, locked in the compartments our secrets have fabricated.

Addiction to Suffering

There is very little alcoholics can hold on to in their addiction except their commitment to their secrets. Consider the reason for this: addiction is supported by secrets, and secrets are supported by addiction. Together with all the rest of our secrets, addiction itself becomes but another monumental secret that extends the maze. In this maze, the idea of recovery can slip away from us (and with a high probability of getting lost entirely).

Both sober and addicted gay men and lesbians often feel caught in a maze created by guilt and shame. They see the world through this ugly grid. The contempt, anger and fear that others exhibit toward them is something they never chose. Nor did they choose to be alcoholics or addicts! And they certainly did *not* choose to be homosexual, or choose the vast array of secrets they use to hide their shame, their guilt, and their rage over their powerlessness to change those who belittle and persecute them. It is these secrets forced on them for survival that turn them into prisoners. What they did choose are their survival tactics, which now, all too often, are their obstacles.

I have visited men in prison and experienced, briefly, the overwhelming sense of frustration and wasted opportunity that penetrates their lives every hour of the day and night. Active alcoholics live in a similar mental and emotional environment. Their secrets incarcerate them in such a way that they begin to react like prisoners condemned to a cell, a cell that grows smaller and smaller as addiction progresses. Addicts, nevertheless, come to depend on their cages in order to survive. Accepting that each of us has chosen the obstacles that will keep us in this cage, many have changed "cages"—from alcohol to pot, from pot to speed, from speed to heroin, or from drugs to food or sex—rather than face anything that threatens this existence.

This is the paradox: the secrets we create to protect ourselves become the bars of our prison! Instead of the safety we thought we had found by hiding behind our secrets, we find at this point in our journey, that they are major obstacles in our path. Pretending they will go away on their own or that they really do not affect our recovery is a step backward into denial. Other people have found this out the hard way.

Because we have lived as if our lives depended on our secrets, we need to be encouraged to understand that our secrets depend on us for their existence. Without us, they vanish. It is our belief that they are so precious to our survival that keeps us stuck in them. Recognizing that we are stuck is a sign of progress, however. Since childhood, the habit of lying has often helped us survive. It is so deep-rooted that even when a friend now asks how we are, we automatically say "Fine!" whether we are or not. How difficult it is to speak the truth, for often we don't know what it is. We honestly don't know how we feel! Unless we see these lies as lies, we do not become willing to do what we must to change.

Looking into the mirror at ourselves, at our lives as we have lived them, is a great deal to ask in early recovery. For those who are determined to find the easier, softer way, it might even be too much. "Haven't I suffered enough in addiction? Why do I need to continue beating up on myself in sobriety?" We support our commitment to recovery through the willingness to trust that the process that has already been laid out will work. We are worth this commitment.

In Step Four, we created an inventory, and I have known many who have suffered tremendously over this effort. They spent weeks and even months developing this list, and their inner turmoil reached towering proportions. For the first time, in a very vivid and dramatic way, they recognized themselves looking at the world through all of their problems. They understood how much everything in their lives was colored and influenced by their secrets, their habits of lying, their survival tactics, and the iron-clad rules they learned to live with in their families.

People use their secrets like drugs and alcohol—to dull their senses and to drown any wish they have to develop their own potential for growth and change. When they are lost to their problems, they have neither the time, the energy or the inclination to make any efforts to work on themselves. Step Four is a task that vigorously confronts this familiar pattern of behavior while, at the same time, encouraging individuals to see themselves exactly as they are.

After years of hiding and pretending, after years of burying feelings beneath a facade of secrets and lies, we can be amazed to discover that we have survived such an insidious campaign of self-sabotage. What we find hidden in the midst of all the emotional rubble is not the "awful-terrible" we thought was there. Instead, we reveal to ourselves a sensitive, caring, abandoned child waiting to be embraced and healed. What a miracle!

Such a heavy price we have paid for our deception! Our secrets, our obstacles, have, over the years, completely taken over the focus of our feelings. In addiction, we have had little or nothing left over for spontaneity or creativity. Most of us are astounded to discover that our patterns of dishonesty are so ingrained that we leap at lying even about things we have no reason to. We lie sooner than we tell the truth because that is what we have learned to do.

Gay men and lesbians protect themselves under a far heavier mantle of secrets then do heterosexuals. Taking Step Four, for us, contradicts everything we have learned about survival. It is especially difficult for us to accept that continued survival and progress in recovery depends on taking this Step. Because it was an effort at private self-disclosure, we were probably willing to begin to work on an inventory; since no one except ourselves was involved, our fears were under control.

Step Four was difficult, but Step Five looms as monumental to most gay men and lesbians in recovery. It is a frontal assault on the forbidden: telling someone else who we really are. Revealing our

secrets to another human being arouses the very feelings of inadequacy we have been tormented by in society, along with the fear and
mistrust of others that never failed to make us drink or use drugs!
"How can you ask us to do such a thing?"

Into the Light

Unless we become willing to share our secrets with another person,
we will continue to use them in the same manner we have used them
in the past. And, sooner or later, the moment will come when we
will reach for the support of alcohol or drugs to make it bearable to
live with them. Writing the list is only the beginning of the process
of stepping out from behind the shadows into the light.

We think we can just put our inventory in a drawer and blithely go
on from there because we fail to assess the power our secrets have
over us. These secrets caused us to live the way we did in the past.
Revealing them to another human being will change our lives in the
present and in the future.

In the past, we faced our lives through both the weaknesses and
the strengths identified in our inventories. We have now seen obstacles as survival tactics and as the source of many of our secrets and
deceptions. It is all there: what we have lived through in the past is
now vividly revealed in the words we have written. And is nothing
changed? Are we are not the same as we have always been?

There are important differences; some we can recognize and others
we cannot. The most obvious change is that we have stopped using
any and all mood-altering substances. Unless we have done this, we
are still deceiving ourselves about the meaning of recovery. Next, the
effects of taking Step One, Step Two, Step Three and Step Four are
continuing, day by day, to penetrate our patterns of behavior. It is
often the case that though we can observe the changes these Steps
have made in others, we cannot clearly see them in ourselves. Pos-
sibly other people have shared their observations of the changes they
have seen in us, and we have been surprised to learn the good news.
Indeed, something is happening within us, and a brief spot check
will reveal some examples:

- We have stopped isolating ourselves and begun relating to others.
- We have begun to take care of our bodies with nutritious food, exercise and rest.
- We have stabilized our sleeping patterns.
- We have started to read again.
- We may have begun to pray or meditate regularly.

Taking a good look at the positive things we are doing in our lives provides us with the information we need.

It is not uncommon to hear recovery spoken of as a "gift." For those of us who have been through the hell of addiction, beginning recovery has been the most precious gift we've ever received, and to continue in recovery is a source of daily gratitude. Maintaining and extending recovery a day at a time is, perhaps, the dearest wish of all for every alcoholic. Hanging on to our secrets will prevent us from experiencing the benefits of these gifts. For any of us to live differently, we need to begin to live without secrets.

Facing Our Fears

At some stage in early recovery, it is not at all uncommon for people to begin to think that they do not deserve sobriety and good health, especially after the kind of lives they have lived. Even after having begun the process, they fear it is a mistake and they cannot be privileged enough to enjoy it for long. This temptation to destroy the benefits they have received is very much part of playing the victim and of the addictive temperament. Waiting for the other shoe to fall, waiting for tragedy to strike, they may themselves actually devise the crisis and the tragedy.

When we are fearful, we attract what will frighten us. When we expect bad things, these things will find their way to us. As long as our self-esteem is in shambles because of what we have done in the past, we are like magnets that continue to attract negative influences into our lives.

Practicing alcoholics and addicts habitually act in negative ways, indulging in thoughts and actions harmful to themselves and to others. To act in positive ways, we must have room to move into a different place in ourselves, into a healthier, sober space. When we are filled with the guilt and shame and rage of the past, there is no alternative except to continue to live with old behavior. Saturated with guilt and shame, we will respond as guilty and ashamed; seething with rage, we will seek and find ways to act out our anger. It is through the effort to clear away all we have collected in the past that we can begin to see the possibility of living in today without such negativity.

We cannot put the past behind us by pretending it does not exist, nor by minimizing it, nor by convincing ourselves we will never live that way again. We must take positive action against the negativity of our past lives. We must confront it. We must go through the experience of feeling what has gone on before, of living through it not as a recitation of "ancient history" but for the experience of what it is like to act and think negatively. Most of us have been in deep denial about our own role in what has happened to us. We need to see this and find a truer perspective. Unless we understand our role, we have no responsibility for changing our thoughts and actions in the future.

Feeling Our Feelings

We are creatures of feeling. Through our feelings, we come to understand ourselves, and others. We can change our habitual behavior by deciding that we no longer wish to have the feelings that come from these actions. We reach this decision after we are clear that we do not value those actions but, instead, choose to value very different ones.

Our minds alone do not change us. Our feelings, our emotions, tell us they do not wish to continue in the same pain. Though our mind can support our choice once we make it, remember that this mind has been seriously affected by the addiction it has endured. It is the mind of an addict—and perhaps an adult child of alcoholic parents as well. We have also damaged our bodies. But each of us has great restorative capabilities. Both the mind and the body can spring back in amazing ways. In order to change, instead of being at cross-purposes with each other, the mind and the body must be linked by the same intention, not going off on their own tangents.

In our addiction, many of us at one time or another made the decision to stop drinking or using. We know what happened with these decisions. Our bodies were chemically dependent, and it was not long before our minds and emotions sought the refuge they knew could be found in the substances we had "given up."

In a Twelve-Step program we found, for the first time, the help essential to get our bodies and our minds to join forces instead of working against each other. Unlike certain recovery programs that substitute the use of some other drug for the one(s) we have used in the past, Twelve-Step programs focus on action. This action restores our minds, our emotions, and our bodies. Instead of chemicals, addicts use their own energies to develop equilibrium through the tools of the program.

The program helps us begin to believe we, ourselves, are capable of recovery. There is no physician in a white coat to hand us still another drug. There is nothing to reinforce the belief that we need to be dependent upon something or someone who can fix us, or that seeking health and recovery is *outside* our own capabilities. The programs carry the message of self-renewal and peer support as we find our way through the wreckage of the past.*

Each of us has a past. What we do about our past is very significant at this point in our journey. By the time we have come to Step Five, we will honestly wish to turn our lives around and turn our negative patterns of thought and action in a positive direction. To do this, we use our lives, as we have come to understand them through the inventory we completed, as the basis for this change. Instead of burying this list in the same way we have always done with our secrets, we need to share it with someone else. The act of sharing the entire inventory with one person is a totally different approach than we have ever taken and, in itself, marks a break with the past.

In admitting to another person what we have done and what we have left undone, we hear our own voice in our ears. Now, the basic

---

*Gay men and lesbians who need hospitalization because their depression is life-threatening, or who cannot stop relapsing, should consider calling the Pride Institute in Minnesota. The Pride Institute offers an inpatient program for lesbians and gay men: 800-54-PRIDE.

idea of taking action—the key to recovery—takes on new meaning. With meaningful action, we suspend our role of victim, of being acted upon, of being incapable of handling life except as a dependent. In positive action, there is progress on the road out of addiction.

Sharing our secrets with another human being is an affirmation of ourselves *by* ourselves. "Yes, I am the one who did this, and this, and that. I own it; this is the way I have lived my life. *And* I can go on from here." We began our journey in denial—"I'm *not* an alcoholic; I'm *not* an addict; I'm *not* gay; I'm *not* a lesbian." We now progress to a place that is new and different for us. When we are willing to take this Step, we experience an unfamiliar burst of self-esteem by saying who we *are* instead of who we aren't. For some of us, it may be the first time in our lives we discover that when we do this the earth does not split open and swallow us! Facing the unfaceable takes courage.

The basis of our denial has been self-delusion, and through self-revelation we reverse this process. A step at a time, instead of escaping into fantasy, we first confront ourselves. We then share this with someone else, a witness, someone outside ourselves. The act takes courage because the honesty we bring to it unlocks the door that we have sealed shut during the period of our addiction: responsibility for ourselves. By accepting responsibility for our secrets as we share them with another, we step into the present. Because we have revealed ourselves as we are, we no longer have to live imprisoned by our secrets. We can begin to use our energy for positive thinking and action.

Admitting our secrets gets them out into the open and creates some space between ourselves and them. This space is exactly what we need to begin to understand that we have a choice in deciding how we will act or think. In sobriety, we always have a choice; in addiction, we think only about our next fix. Yes, that is the way we have lived in the past. That was one of our secrets. And we have learned that others have hidden the same thing. In recovery, none of us has to hide his or her addiction, and because we don't hide it, it no longer controls our lives.

We cannot change anything for today unless we understand the way we have been yesterday. Taking Step Five acknowledges to ourselves and to someone else our old patterns of thought and action. If, in fact, we no longer value the way we have lived in the past, we now have the opportunity to make different choices.

Processing Our Own Material

The Twelve-Step programs use a very basic approach that accelerates recovery. With the help of others like ourselves, we find encouragement to begin to process our own material. In the meetings, in the presence of other people, we begin to gain some new insights into how we have done things in the past, and ways in which we can look at our lives from a different perspective. We initiate healthy approaches to living and working when we show up to process this material—to identify it, to understand it, to clear it out, to make way for new information. It is difficult to do this because we have become so used to living with the wreckage of the past. We have structured our inner "houses" and the furnishings of each day with it, and we count on it for support. When we begin recovery, we feel as if we have moved into a new "house" with all of the old "furniture." This is hard to see with any clarity, except through others. Other people's habits and priorities are much easier to discern and judge than our own.

In Step Five, we take direct action to end the stagnation that frequently sets in after attending meetings and listening to other people who are trying to stay sober and clean one day at a time. We need to examine our own habits, our own priorities, our own obstacles in order for us to become clearer about them.

There is no right way to take this fifth Step. A few suggestions about it may be helpful:

- The person you choose to listen to your inventory should be someone with whom you can be as vulnerable and as safe as possible.
- With someone you can trust in this way, give yourself permission to honestly review your life.
- Schedule enough time, several hours at least, in which to go over the inventory. Don't rush through it.

- Choose a place in which you have a sense of privacy. Some public places, like a park or a quiet restaurant, may also provide an excellent setting.
- Begin with what you have written, and add additional things when these occur to you. Talk about your thoughts and feelings as you proceed.
- Feel your feelings: let them be OK with you.
- Accept whatever comments are offered to you at the time instead of negating them with "Yes, but. . ."
- Remember, this is not a perfect inventory. Many people take a fifth Step every eighteen months or so, just to review unfinished business from their past that comes up in recovery.
- Bear in mind there is nothing impossible or too terrible to reveal; your recovery depends on sharing everything you can.
- Allow yourself to trust in the process, and go on from there.

Most gay men and lesbians have almost no experience with the privilege of revealing themselves. For many, it is the first time in their lives that they have an opportunity like this, and the element of threat is very real. "You'll hate me once you know what I'm really like." "How can I go on living my old ways once you know all about me?" The fear of rejection and the fear of change, losing the little we think we've got, are powerful inhibitions for us. By doing the fifth Step with one person, we learn that it is safe to tell our secrets, and that we will not be rejected because of them. With this experience behind us, we can move on to share honestly at the group level and to know a broader acceptance.

During our lifetime, both prior to and during addiction, many of us have made foolish choices of people to confide in. It seems that, with a few exceptions, we have turned to those we could absolutely count on to criticize, punish (in some way), and reject us. We have chosen the ones who were the least able to accept us as we are, and who never failed to rush in to change us, "fix" us, make us some other way. If this is not a pattern for you, then you have been very fortunate and will have no difficulty deciding with whom you will take Step Five. Others will have to consider carefully the people who are available.

In many cases, the obvious choice is one's sponsor. Some may prefer a different person, an individual who is outside the daily routine of life. However, we choose a sponsor to support our recovery; chances are that the decision to review our inventory with this person is a healthy extension of this decision. It is a good idea to put one's sponsor at the top of the list of the people to choose from.

What if we do not have a sponsor? Many gay men and lesbians avoid getting a sponsor because of a deeply rooted fear of intimacy. The possibility of rejection is so intense that they avoid using this valuable program tool to aid their recovery. Instead, they rely entirely on literature, meetings, and telephone calls to a vast array of friends with whom they can share a piece here and a piece there, but never the whole story in one place. We need to take Step Five with one other person, and if the question of intimacy hasn't arisen before this, it will certainly come up at this time.

There is no way around it; we cannot take this Step alone. That is why the Step is introduced at this place in our journey. We could work on any of the first four Steps on our own, and for many of us, working in isolation was a basic part of our pattern. Now, however, we need another person to review our inventory with, and that changes everything. It is a risk that we *must* take, and it tests the limits of our recovery to the fullest.

It is not a good idea to rely entirely upon intellect to make this decision. In recovery, I've discovered for myself that I have been able to tune in to my intuition more and more as time went on. In our addiction, there is no one home to listen; in recovery, we become available to the good counsel that we have stored away and are now able to give ourselves. We begin to listen to and develop trust in our own counsel the longer we are clean and sober. This is one of the most heartening rewards of our new way of living in recovery.

With help from our own intuition, we can make the best decision regarding the sharing of our inventory. It may, indeed, be with someone outside a Twelve-Step program. It may be a counselor, therapist, or member of the clergy. I have also known people to take this Step with a total stranger. The point is that we actually choose to reveal ourselves to another human being—and to God/HP—instead of burying our past. If we are ready to confront other issues—like intimacy, fear of rejection, fear of the consequences of honesty—then we will choose someone to listen who can support us.

Taking this Step with the right person neutralizes our own negativity. No matter what we thought of our actions, in revealing them a certain kind of dilution occurs. Perhaps our listener shares something from his or her own past that is similar to our experience or else acknowledges our courage for being willing to make such a revelation. In place of the void that always seemed to be waiting, we connect with the world in a way that we hadn't before. Nothing is too bad or too terrible to be told to another human being, but we never would have believed this until we actually did it ourselves!

The catharsis that is possible is vitally important to recovery. Our secrets have functioned exclusively in our imagination without any larger frame of reference. In revealing our secrets to another, we set up a scale on which we can balance the worst that we believed against the entire gamut of human action. We experience the movement of life through *all* actions, and instead of being "the worst culprits in the world" (that is, "the center of the universe"), we discover who we really are. We lose our uniqueness in the discovery that we are more *like* others than we are different from them.

Instead of living as if we were separate and special and without any share in the chain of humanity, gay and lesbian recovering alcoholics can come to understand, through taking this Step, that we are people, like other people. We can choose to use our energy in a positive way just as we made the choice to use it negatively in the past. This is the decision we must make now. In this Step in which we reveal to another what our life has been, we clear space in which we can begin to think and act positively. In the swirling storm of negativity, it is not possible to find our way through the maze of secrets and dishonesty. If we will allow Step Five to set our feet on cleared and solid ground, we will find our way out of the labyrinth.

GUIDES TO PROGRESS

"I'm *afraid* to ask anyone to be my sponsor. It's not something I can do—it's just not me." Tom had just suggested that Karen do this for the eleven-millionth time since they had met at a gay and lesbian sober picnic in the park.

"Well, no one can make you do it; it's your program. You'd sure find it a lot easier if you'd get one," said Tom.

"Why would it be easier? Just tell me why?" asked Karen.

"A sponsor is one of the most important tools available to us. You've learned how you can work on the Steps, read the literature, and go to meetings and share with other people; you know how all of these work for you. A sponsor is an additional tool, not an obstacle to your recovery," Tom answered.

"I never thought of it like that. If everything else is working for me, why wouldn't having a sponsor work, as well? OK, how about you? Will you be my sponsor?"

"Sure," laughed Tom, "I'll be your *temporary* sponsor—until you can find another lesbian to work with you on some issues that only she can help you with. Thanks for asking me."

"Thanks for getting me started," said Karen with a hug.

David had been out of touch with his family for almost a year, and he wanted to call his mother because it was her birthday the following week. She, as well as his father, always asked so many questions about his life. Although he wasn't ready yet to come out to them as a gay man, he wanted to let them know he had almost nine months in recovery. "They always smother me when we talk, and I don't want that to happen. Have you ever had a situation like this?" he asked his sponsor, Sam.

"Parents are at the top of my list of button-pushers. They know where to find every one of them, and you know where to find their buttons, as well. If you want to be in touch without being over-whelmed, you might want to send a card or a letter. Or, if you really did want to call, you could always make it clear that this was only to wish her a happy birthday and to tell her you were no longer drinking or using. If she begins on anything else, just say that you'll have to get back to her in a few weeks—when you're ready to discuss those other issues. Instead of saying yes or no to anything I'm not ready for, all I say is 'Let me get back to you,' or 'I need some time to think about that.' It works for me. Let me know how it works for you."

"Thanks, Sam. I'll call her tonight and tell you what happens."

Suggestions for Action

An easy and inexpensive way of being nice to ourselves after a stressful day, or just because we need to give ourselves a treat, is to take a warm bath—with or without bubbles—and listen to some pleasant music. Let the answering machine take calls, and for an added dimension, light a candle or two, and allow the candlelight and the music and the warm water in the tub to relax you.

REFLECTIONS

We stand at a crossroads in our lives when we become available to accepting and loving ourselves.

Step Six

"THAT'S HOW I AM!"

CONDITION: INFLEXIBILITY

The alcoholic is an expert doormat when it comes to people-pleasing, and as rigid as a brick about following the rules developed in the past, rejecting new approaches to living, or relinquishing the role of victim. All sense of security depends upon hanging on to inflexibility. There is not the slightest possibility of changing this attitude; we never have permission to make mistakes. It is weakness to flinch from this position, and only the "strong" survive. Meanwhile, life grows more and more unmanageable.

ALTERNATIVE: FLEXIBILITY

Manipulation, the fine art in which the addict is skilled, will not work in recovery. Changing staterooms on the last voyage of the *Titanic* did not get any passenger off a ship that was already under way. We implement real change by putting into practice what we have assimilated through the first five Steps. By giving ourselves permission *not* to have the answers and to make as many mistakes as we need to, we begin to live on life's terms.

STEP SIX:

Were entirely ready to have God remove all these defects of character.

Continuing upon this journey into recovery, we discover we have already begun a process of change. We no longer see ourselves solely from the perspective of gay and lesbian alcoholics living lost to our addiction. We are beginning to take a different look at the society in whose midst we have lived our closeted or uncloseted lives. The efforts we have made so far have provided us with a new understanding of ourselves. Life in the wilderness of early recovery has helped us to appreciate that it is one thing to *live* in the desert and another to *be*, inside ourselves, a desert.

We lose all perspective in the desert. Every grain of sand blazes, and the fire of the sun is everywhere. Those courageous ones who decide to examine themselves in this desert have discovered things about themselves and others they never considered possible. The most incredible discovery of all, perhaps, is that even in this blazing furnace love *of* and *for* others, and oneself, can exist, and that no intensity of heat can destroy this love.

As we worked first to identify, and then to begin to accept our lives and how we have lived them in the past, we learned a great deal about the individual we are *not*. In this process, we observed many things we were critical about in ourselves and others. Though none of this changes anything about the past, we established a conscious link *with* the past. This link is very important if we wish to work on changing ourselves in the present. By identifying what we need to work at, we can develop abilities to handle these matters. If we discover we do not have the necessary skills, we can then choose to learn them.

Understanding Our Obstacles

Unfortunately, the opposite can also happen. We may discover things about ourselves that we believed we knew or understood but, in fact, did not. Our refusal to accept these can provide more obstacles for us: we do not learn what we do not accept as important for us. That is why writing down the inventory of our obstacles, our "secrets," was so important. It documented what we currently know and understand about ourselves. From this inventory, we see the basis for our rigidity, our inflexibility. This list is exactly what we were referring to when we said in the past to others, "This is how I am. Take it or leave it!" Let's take a closer look at the obstacles that make us the way we are.

We conceive of obstacles from our own limited, personal focus, our private habits of thinking. What may seem significant to us, because of our unique perspective as gay men and lesbians, can frequently be insignificant to others—and vice versa. Understanding obstacles in all their dimensions is the key to using them to help us instead of to thwart us. Instead of seeing them as walling us off from the future, preventing our growth and happiness, it is important that we begin to see them as opportunities waiting for us, like fields, to till and plant for the harvest of tomorrow. When we approach them with this attitude, we change the way they appear to us.

Consider the example of waves crashing on a beach. Instead of perceiving them as attacking and invading the land, think of them as a wall of force that holds the ocean back from the land. Sometimes, a greater force breaks through the wall from the ocean depths, and, when this happens, there is a flood. But seen as a wall, the waves that ring the shoreline *contain* the ocean. Our obstacles contain us for as long as we exert no effort to pass beyond them.

What we now see as obstacles are made so by our present level of understanding about ourselves. We have created the walls through which we must pass by our own concepts of limitation or capability. Instead of seeing obstacles as permanent and absolute, "for ever and ever," we can begin to allow ourselves to consider them as "qualities," like colors that, in a different light, may appear to be entirely different. Obstacles—and opportunities—are the products of our understanding. We have been given the opportunities we now have in early recovery to assist our understanding to go beyond itself, to pass beyond our obstacles.

There are no obstacles too difficult for us to overcome. When we become willing to put forth the effort and energy it requires to work on them, we reach a different understanding of their nature. In our addiction, we endured and suffered rather than launch any kind of action against obstacles. When we do begin to act, however, many of us are shocked to discover that it is not the first time we have encountered these same obstacles. They have always stood in the way of a higher level of self-understanding. When an obstacle is put behind us, that level on which we stood is also, miraculously, behind us. We learn this only after we have reached the new perspective.

We have been held hostage by our obstacles during our addiction. Our progress so far on the journey has made us keenly aware of this. Until this time, we have accepted our predicament as gay and lesbian alcoholics who have been killing ourselves in a prison of our own construction. Many of us now come face to face with a desperate dilemma: in all of our pain and our suffering, can we remove our shackles now that we have the choice? Prison is a safe place for those who choose it. Freedom can be terrifying unless we are prepared to face life with new and healthy patterns of behavior that support recovery. With the realization that we need to learn these new ways, we begin to understand that this opportunity is present for us when we begin work on Step Six.

Our Old Rules

For gay men and lesbians, there is no more prevalent pattern than that of seeing ourselves as victims. In addiction, as we have already observed, this attitude was merely intensified and made more indelible. In order to understand change in recovery we need a totally different perspective; we need to work at changing the idea of ourselves as victims. This basic attitude is at the very center of the way we have conceived of—and lived—our lives.

From the time we were children, we developed life skills crucial for our survival. We began developing these skills when we first discovered we were in trouble. Perhaps we noticed other children were not attracted by the things that attracted us, or perhaps we played roles that did not seem to fit us, or it is even possible that we had feelings of interest or desire for someone of the same sex. No matter what the cause, we felt there was something different, something unique, about us that needed to be protected from others.

The next step in the process of victimization was the development of rules that made it possible to hide our feelings. We never did this, or that, in front of others, because it would give us away. We always pretended that we liked to do X when the truth was that we really wanted to do Y. We "stuffed" our feelings, we pretended they did not exist, and tried never to expose them to ridicule or punishment. We learned not to share with others who we really were, or what we really felt.

These rules helped us to survive as children and as adolescents in our homes, and as adults in the heterosexual world. Even when we ventured out of the closet among other gay men and lesbians, our basic rules still worked the rest of the time. By sticking with our rules, we have set ourselves up to suffer as victims for the rest of our lives—even in recovery! The process of healing involves the willingness to revise these rules that no longer work, even though we cannot predict the consequences of such radical action on our lives. Our rules have made us victims; therefore, we must become willing to change these rules.

Alcoholics are expert doormats when it comes to people pleasing and as rigid as bricks when it comes to their own rules: "This is how I do this." "This is the way it is done." Rigidity is actually a symptom of addictive patterns of behavior, and instead of attempting to suppress it, we need to examine it. Symptoms are an indication that something is out of balance; contrary to the way in which many of us have looked at symptoms, they are not the cause of the problem.

In recovery, it makes an enormous difference how we look at and evaluate our survival tactics, which, in the words of Step Six, are our "defects of character." Recognizing these symptoms as valuable information instead of being afraid of them is of great help in healing ourselves. Each entry on our inventory marks the way forward on our journey. Unfortunately, this is not how most people see symptoms.

We have survived because of our rules and suffered from them as well. Our rules supported and sustained our survival tactics, our survival tactics carried out the instructions from the rules. Support for living any differently has never been part of our experience. Now we stand looking back at lives strewn with the heavy burden of the rules and survival tactics we have collected all these years. We see that they won't fit through the new doorway of recovery. At the same time that we may feel angry that we've carried them around for so long, we fear what will happen when we leave them behind. Anger and fear—the story of our lives! A sense of sadness overwhelms us when we think of the wasted time and energy we have expended only to come to this moment in which we understand that our lives can't work in the old way. This realization can be truly painful—if we will allow ourselves to feel it!

Perhaps the only comfort we can have, at this time, is to acknowledge how disloyal we have been to ourselves all these years, how we have denied our feelings and chosen victimhood. Somehow, the terrible emptiness inside coalesces when we do this, and some little murmur of support for ourselves living honestly filters up. We are children learning to become adults. Our illusions have backed a step away from us, and we have a little space in which we can see them for what they are. We need to go on from here either with them—or without them. We may honestly have no idea what it would mean to be loyal to ourselves, and that is OK. We can learn.

I remember hearing a man speak about this place we reach in ourselves . "Yo' mamma ain't commin'!" is the refrain he used over and over again as he told me his story. It still rings in my ears when I think about Step Six. No one else can do anything about *my* obstacles; no one else can dissolve *my* inflexibility. I am the only one who can become willing to change. But this will not happen for me unless I am willing to come out from behind my victimhood and live as if I am entitled to a healthy, happy life as a valuable member—a valuable gay or lesbian member—of society! My mamma ain't comin', but I don't need her to rescue me anymore! I can do it myself, together with you, and we can help each other.

Heterosexuals in recovery already feel themselves to be members of society. Gay men and lesbians have the difficult task of coming out from behind their victimhood before they know what this feeling is like. Becoming ready to work on eradicating "defects of character" involves no longer allowing these to be special limitations arising out of our sexual orientation but the kind of shortcomings that every human being who becomes an addict has. Straight addicts and alcoholics have acted almost exactly the same way gay men and lesbians have; their obstacles are neither greater nor smaller than ours. Healing ourselves means believing this. Healing ourselves means becoming flexible about changing our rules for survival.

Valuing Sobriety

During our addiction, when all we truly valued was drugs, or alcohol, or compulsive sex, or compulsive eating, we filled our lives with these. When we begin to value our sobriety and our abstinence, we begin to choose support for freedom from the addictive conditions that used to wreck our lives.

We may ask ourselves, What is it we have come to value in the wilderness of early recovery through which we have journeyed? Considering this question carefully, it becomes clear that we have constantly compared our experience with what our lives had been before we began in recovery. Our minds have set up the comparisons, and we have experienced recovery in the reflection of these images from the past. Even in the wilderness, the values from our dead-ended lives in addiction have been our baggage. Didn't we begin recovery in order to end the despair, the isolation, the bondage of addiction? If we truly wish for a new beginning, we must work on ending the comparisons with what has been, even though we have no idea what life will be like when we do this. We must now be willing to change even though we do not understand what that means.

In the wilderness, we live in the desert of our dreams, the tangle of cross-purposes, the paradox of life as we thought it would be compared with life as it actually is. We are in a crucible in which forces beyond our control pummel us from all sides. In it, we seek a place to begin structuring our future. In the past, we may have believed we knew where we were going and how we were going to get there, even if we never admitted it to ourselves. In the wilderness, we face the truth that in order to change, we do *not* know where we are going or how to find the way. This is the opposite extreme from knowing all the answers.

Our Survival

Allowing ourselves to examine without any delusions our former goals and our approaches to them, we understand that we must have help if we are to find our path to a new way of living. How ironic to recognize this need so soon after becoming convinced that we cannot trust our own power to move ahead! This is an opportunity for us to observe, once again, our powerlessness over all addictions. At the same time we see that, we understand the rest much more clearly than before: accessing our power means that we will have to make ourselves available to assistance from sources deep within, as well as beyond, ourselves. Only after we have come to believe that such help, such support, exists are we able to allow ourselves to receive it.

As children, this is exactly what we did. We were powerless amid parents and other grown ups who exerted their influence on us. Many have tasted the bitterness that comes from expecting more from these power sources than they were able, or had adequate intelligence, to provide. The fact is, we survived by trusting almost no one but ourselves. Nevertheless, we did it; we survived.

In the wilderness, we experience the failure, the bankruptcy, of our own power as we have used it in the past and come to realize that others can help us find a new way to proceed. Whether or not we wish to identify this power as God, "good orderly direction," HP, or the group, it has been possible to recognize that the child within us can allow other people to help. Even the most unbelieving of us has lived through childhood, and this experience is invaluable in recovery. We have encountered others here in recovery who we know can help us.

Whatever isolation and despair we have felt, now and in the past, has been linked with the isolation and despair that these others have shared with us. Because they have been able to survive it, we have connected with the hope that we, too, can survive. Even now, they support us in the belief that we can continue to survive. Some of us may be able to observe in them a Higher Power working in their lives. Identifying with them, we can admit the possibility of change entering their lives, and, with this admission, ours as well. If others have been able to make themselves available to help after all that has happened to them, then it is possible we may be able to also.

We certainly have every reason to be afraid. We have lived without expecting help for so long that we do not know how to act now or what its effect on us will be. That is why this period is so valuable! In it, we begin to learn the basics; we learn that we are beginners - (children) - again, and that it is OK to act like children: teachable. In adulthood, it is very difficult to become teachable; as adults, we are convinced that either we have the answers already or we *should* have the answers. We are in denial about *not* having the answers. In early recovery, we are no longer able to deceive ourselves about this.

It is terribly important to remember not to be in a hurry to leave this vulnerable state. When we leave it without adequate preparation, the old habits quickly return. If we are concerned with change, real change, we need to know that the greatest changes of all are made *in* the wilderness. The question, then, is, How much do we wish to change? In this vulnerable place, we can confront this question in our most teachable mode.

Being alone here is only an illusion. This has become clearer and clearer as we journey on. Our past isolation was the result of the way in which we used our energy, the things we chose to value, and the secrets we hid from others and ourselves. Acknowledging that we need help to change these, and witnessing these changes in other people's lives, we have begun to understand that help is available. We have come to accept this even as we observe it, and the infusion of it in our lives provides us with convincing evidence that we are not alone.

Even more help has come to us in our observation of it flowing to others: we are like them; they are like us. Our self-esteem takes an enthusiastic leap upward when we discover, to our amazement, that we can be the source of help to others who are just beginning the journey. After the ordeals we have been through, that we are now capable of helping others seems miraculous.

Many people in early recovery throw themselves wholeheartedly into helping other newcomers, and they are quite surprised to discover themselves caught up in some old patterns of thinking and acting. Giving other people advice, "taking their inventory" as it is called, is much easier than working on changing oneself! Having taken Steps Four and Five, we have provided ourselves with exactly what we need in order to change ourselves: *our own inventories*. Instead of directing our efforts toward other people's inventories—indulging in the critical habits from our past—we can now focus on our own.

As experts on ourselves, we need to use our inventories as advice to ourselves on what we need to focus on in order to change. Reviewing our inventories with another person, as we have done, has brought our secrets out of the darkness of denial and into a new light; now we have the opportunity to begin working on the substance of our own material in a new space. We understand, at last, that this is no longer someone else's program. This is our own prescription for change.

Is there any word more threatening that *change*? Even for those of us who believe we truly want it, the idea of change is limited by what we already know and rarely, if ever, completely open-ended.

When we think about what our lives could be like outside of our addiction, we use as a frame of reference our lives *before* we became substance abusers. For some, this was childhood or adolescence; nevertheless, as unrealistic as it may seem, these memories are often the only basis we have for the comparison.

Most of us realize that, as adults, we cannot live as we did in childhood. Because we do not yet know sober, new, alternatives, we may struggle with grave uncertainties and an inexplicable sense of misgiving about the future. These feelings frequently remind us of our lives in addiction, and many people find themselves questioning the value of being clean and sober but still tormented by these fears.

Unless encouraged to do otherwise, we will continue to respond with old patterns of behavior. The pull of old associations with people, places and things from the past will exert powerful influence on us in our newly discovered sobriety. Having lived for years only with the support of other gay men or lesbians—without the support of families, professional associations, the acceptance of society in general—gay people in recovery often suffer deeply from the loss of gay friends who are still practicing their addictions. We feel, even in recovery, like victims. This time, we are victims of change. For us, change has always meant we have nowhere to go and no one to go with. This is how it may feel, even though the opposite is true.

Living in recovery is not easy. We have learned, as far as we have come, that the only way to do it is through action. It is not possible to stand still: we either move toward or away from the drink or the drug or the other substances or behavior to which we were addicted. The Twelve-Step programs are action programs. The action we are willing to take to let go of old patterns of addictive behavior supports our recovery efforts.

The Two-Way Street

Our efforts so far have helped us to understand that we are surrounded with help on all sides. Nothing has occurred to alter this understanding, not even taking Step Five, the sharing of our inventories with another person. Most of us, after taking this Step, have experienced a taste of freedom previously unknown to us. We have shared this with others. We have also been willing to lend our support to newcomers and to take on ourselves the tasks that needed to be performed at our home-group meetings. Whether we have gone to gay or straight meetings, a deeper understanding of our value as recovering alcoholics has dawned on us.

Each step we have taken has increased the value of other people for us, and by the same mathematics, of ourselves to them. As we have become more and more willing to change, we have become more and more valuable in supporting others in their efforts to change. Recovery, unlike the dead end of addiction, has become a two-way thoroughfare on which we all journey together.

In the Twelve-Step programs, one of the miracles people often speak about is the incredible feeling of love and gratitude they experience when they first enter the meetings. "It is so real, you can almost reach out and touch it!" someone once said. When we begin to participate, we begin the process of change that makes us available to working all the Steps of the program.

None of us has done it alone; help has come to us all along the way. It would be a mistake for us now to forget that. Just as we have received this support for the first five Steps of the journey, it is there for us for Step Six as well. We no longer have to do anything by ourselves, in isolation. That is one of the promises of the program. Therefore, becoming "entirely ready" is a task we can work on with the support of our sponsors, our friends in and out of Twelve-Step programs, the literature we read, and our prayers and meditations. When we are willing to honestly say who we are and what it is we need, and when we are available to receive it, we are no longer victims of either our addiction or the society in which we live.

GUIDES TO PROGRESS

"I'm really going crazy about this. No matter where I go or what I do, all I can think about is sex. I was never this horny when I was drinking! What the hell is wrong with me?" Guy had finally got up enough nerve to talk about a problem that had been bugging him for weeks.

The three other men sitting at the table in the restaurant after the Twelve-Step meeting all shook their heads. "I know what that's like," said Gary.

"Me too," said Paul.

"It's weird, isn't it? You get clean and sober only to get crazy over sex!" said Jim.

"The one thing that really worked for me was giving myself permission not to have sex for three months. It seemed to cool me down," said Gary.

"I handled it myself," laughed Jim, along with the other three men.

"Well, it got me thinking about the rest of my life and the way I was hooked on anonymous sex. I started going to Sex and Love Addicts Anonymous meetings and began using the Twelve Steps to learn to live with myself," said Paul.

"You mean there's hope for me?" asked Guy.

"You're sharing it with us right now? Be sure you take some of it home with you," answered Jim.

Margie had not had a drink or used drugs for over a year, and still she was going through terrible mood swings. She started having anxiety attacks that pounced on her without warning, and headaches that persisted for days, and she was more and more uncomfortable trying to fit in clothes that had become too tight for her. "Have you been to see your doctor recently, Margie?" asked Ellen, her new sponsor.

"What for? I've got the program, and you. What do I need a doctor for?"

"It's a good idea to have a checkup soon after getting started in recovery. We've all put our bodies through hell during our addiction, so it's important to get a status report on what's working and what isn't. Lots of us have complications related to alcoholism and drug use. Some of us may even have a condition that directly fed into how we became addicted—like diabetes or low blood sugar."

"Do you really think I need to go?" asked Margie.

"Wouldn't it be better to find out so you could do something about it instead of suffering?" answered Ellen. Margie went for a checkup and discovered she had hypoglycemia, a condition she was able to treat with careful attention to diet and stress. Margie's mood swings and headaches stopped, and everything in her entire wardrobe now fits her beautifully as she enters her third year of recovery.

Suggestions for Action

It is much easier to see changes occurring in others than in ourselves. One of the best ways of identifying change within ourselves is by keeping an account of our feelings and our reactions to what goes on around us, day by day. Looking back over the journal he began to write six months before, Tom commented to me, "The guy who wrote that was one sick puppy! I didn't know it then, but I do now." Keeping a journal can help us stay in touch with where we've been in our journey.

REFLECTIONS

How good it is to be open to what once was not there for us; how good it is to live in all the rooms of our house and let the light shine in from all sides.

THE PARADOX OF ARROGANCE

CONDITION: ARROGANCE

Having all the answers is a way of life that doesn't yield easily. In addiction, this attitude is one of the few ways gay men and lesbians know how to protect themselves. But arrogance, grandiosity, unapproachability all encourage isolation and self-doubt. Beneath arrogance lurks the constant fear of being found out and losing everything.

ALTERNATIVE: HUMILITY

Instead of self-centeredness, "self-caringness." We begin to observe the effects of this shift in other people's lives and gradually identify with this attitude.

Real humility is very different from false humility; we can choose now to take pride in being a member of the human race *and* gay. We accept the "invitation" of those in recovery and experience the incredible power of the fellowship, which exceeds any single individual. We learn to turn to this power for help in removing the very obstacles that sustained arrogance.

STEP SEVEN:

Humbly asked God to remove our shortcomings.

We did not become alcoholics in a day; everything in our lives has taken place over time. It takes time to change the way we think and act, and this is true in recovery as well as in addiction. The Steps we have been taking have prepared the way, as well as being themselves the path of change. We have encountered many distractions and tangents so far, and we can be certain that there will be many more ahead of us. Expecting them is helpful, because our progress depends on our willingness to face these difficulties and setbacks in recovery.

Change Agents

Finding other gay men and lesbians to make the journey with us through our Twelve-Step program has been very supportive. The discovery of ourselves as important to others in their progress in recovery introduced a major change in our understanding of how to begin to relate with adults in sobriety. Many of us hadn't a clue about how to act with anyone unless we had alcohol or drugs to depend on. No matter what our chronological age, in recovery we have often felt like children or, at best, adolescents, in social settings. Through the programs, through the meetings and talking on the telephone with a sponsor or with others, we have begun to develop some of the interpersonal skills we lacked or struggled with in the past. As awkward as we felt, we learned that others felt awkward too, and the mutual support did great things for our self-esteem.

At some point farther down the road, when we look back at this period, we will be able to better understand what we have come through. Now, it may appear only strange and confusing. Later on, it will appear natural, and we will see ourselves as being natural in it. By then, we will have discarded more of our "disguises," and we will be wearing our own faces and our own clothes. When we are dressed in our own clothes, we appear as we are. This is of great help in the evolution of our sobriety. Now, we are passing from who-we-have-been-in-the-past to who-we-will-be-in-the-future. It takes time to find "clothes" to fit, and it also takes time to stop feeling so awkward and uncomfortable.

All this happens a little at a time. Small revelations will sometimes appear when we least expect them, and these will grow in significance as additional insights fall into place. For me, these experiences are like sitting in a planetarium with my life projected on the ceiling. From time to time, as if with a touch of a switch, moments from the past or the present suddenly move millions of light-years closer. Our journey has been a process of looking at ourselves, but what we have observed is still so far off that we cannot appreciate all that is there. Day by day, we have been moving out into an adventure with ourselves that knows no limit. We are beginning only gradually to experience and share the excitement we feel about lives no longer lost in the secrets of addiction.

Such a change! Being excited about life instead of about our next "fix"! We even look different, if we will believe what others have told us. We are amazed at how much our physical condition has improved. Food actually tastes different now, and we have begun to feel steadier on our feet. Cups and glasses no longer tremble in our hands. Our bodies are being transformed along with our emotions and our minds.

When we change how we live and what we do with our energy, we modify our own structure. If we act no differently today from the way we acted yesterday, there is no basis for change. But through our efforts at working on recovery, if we perform in new ways and think new thoughts, we become ourselves catalysts of change. Each modification makes it more and more possible to continue in new ways. We are changed by what we do, and others see the changes in us that our actions have created.

It is a grave temptation to stop here, to settle for a limit to recovery. "If it works, don't fix it," is a comment I have often heard to justify such a decision. A comment like that one comes straight out of our old habit of denial, and we need to be honest about this. We have been used to settling for the least most of our lives; early recovery is a long way up from the bottom, so why not get off here? Many people who have done this have discovered how fragile and vulnerable they are and how much power the old addictive patterns of behavior still have on them. Unless we are continually using our energy and attention to work on recovery, we slip back again into addiction before we even realize it.

When we are willing to face the truth about our fear of change instead of slipping back into denial, we get back on track. Without any answers for ourselves or for others, without any pretense about our ability to manage our own lives entirely on our own, without any drugs or alcohol or other substances or compulsive habits to escape into, we can take a look at ourselves, and we can experience, perhaps for the first time, what it means to be humble.

In addiction, we were rarely associated with the trait of humility. Besides being intensely egocentric, most of us were frequently grandiose* and very demanding—especially when it came to the way we felt others should behave toward us. Even when we hit bottom, we had vivid moments of righteous indignation about how miserably we were treated.

For most alcoholics, and especially gay men and lesbians, humility has meant "humiliation" and "degradation," and we have had more than our share. Whether, in our addiction, we reached a low bottom or a high bottom, the experience of humiliation was usually what shocked us into doing something about our condition. Pride, if nothing else, was the lifeline that hauled many of us into a Twelve-Step program. Many people in recovery have shared the same reaction: "I couldn't stand myself any longer." "I got sick and tired of being sick and tired." "When I found myself doing something I swore never to do, I knew I needed help!" "I might as well have died—if I was going to live like that!" "I wasn't human anymore; I hated myself for being such an animal."

Pride has saved many lives. If "humility" meant only the opposite of "pride," many of us would be unable to survive. With our chin on the floor, we'd never make our way even in recovery! Let's accept that being humble means *much more* than acting the opposite of proud.

When we talk with others who came into recovery programs about the same time we did, or those who have come in afterward, we often sense something we cannot put our finger on. When we sit in meetings and listen to gay men and lesbians share some of the incre-

---

*Bill F., who worked years ago at the Seaman's Institute in New York, gave the basic definition of "grandiose" when he described the guy who staggered into his office in a seedy overcoat, three days' growth of beard on his chin and a bottle of Schenley sticking out of his pocket. The individual proceeded to lay down all the conditions on which he would accept help. When these conditions weren't met in precisely the way he said, he walked out refusing all help.

dible hardships they have endured in their lives as children, adolescents and adults, we can be touched with something that is different from sympathy, though we don't know exactly what to call it. When we see hundreds of gay people marching in the streets behind the banners SOBER AND GAY in the Gay Pride parades and the national demonstrations advocating gay rights, we can feel something else there riding the wave of pride that lifts our hearts. And when thousands of clean and sober gay men and lesbians gather at the regional, national or international conferences of Twelve-Step programs, we can be overwhelmed with gratitude for the experience of participating in such an exhilarating response to life.

None of us has done it alone. All of us can feel humble in the presence of something at work far beyond any single individual's capability. In the past, many of us have lived our lives lost to the shame of being gay, as well as being alcoholics or addicts. In the midst of these new experiences in which tens, hundreds, and thousands of us show up to take pride in being gay and in being in recovery, we can also feel deep humility before the power that has brought about such a miracle for all of us—and society—to experience.

"No Pain; No Gain"

Where did we start from? "Keeping it green," as it is called, reminds us of the lives we lived as addicts. Unless we remember, it is easy to lose the perspective we have reached. Without a point of reference, we slip into comparisons with others, which often prove dangerous and even destructive. Even identifying oneself as "My name is _____ and I am an alcoholic," is a way of touching base with one's own progress. It is not, as I once heard suggested, an effort to continue living in the past.*

---

*I have met professional therapists not in recovery who object to people referring to themselves as alcoholics or addicts because they believe labeling is unhealthy. From what I have observed, it is the people who are still practicing their addiction who are unhealthy, and only those who have admitted their addiction who are in recovery. To be more accurate, as well as more supportive of the effort to change, it may be helpful to add the word *recovering* when identifying yourself in a Twelve-Step meeting.

These words are not an attempt to extend the suffering we have experienced. Instead, they acknowledge the pain that alcoholics know is still waiting for them in addiction—should they decide to turn back on their journey into recovery. "Pain is inevitable; suffering is optional." This is one of the slogans repeated at meetings. Another slogan is "No pain; no gain." Both slogans remind us of truths vital to our recovery—that we are only human, that we are vulnerable even in our sobriety, that we must go through our obstacles if we are to overcome them.

Pain is one thing that deflates everyone's ego. It is the great leveler. Goliaths and Amazons have been humbled by pain. A significant part of our expertise about ourselves relates directly to the pain we have known prior to and in our addiction. The Twelve-Step programs have encouraged us to learn new ways to deal with pain instead of turning to drugs. These are some of the ways people in recovery manage pain:

- Make a list of basic needs, expectations, and goals at this moment.
- Use the Serenity Prayer and other prayers or meditations we have learned.
- Work the Steps of the program.
- Share the pain with someone else either face to face, or over the telephone.
- Listen to the "places" inside ourselves that call out for support and comfort; acknowledge them.
- Dispel any guilt or shame over feeling pain; pain is the sound of an alarm going off, and we are wise to heed it.
- Avoid activities, physical, emotional or mental, that will intensify or extend the pain.
- Instead of rejecting ourselves for being in pain, embrace ourselves, lovingly, like children who are hurt and need attention.
- Remind ourselves that the pain will pass, that it is not forever, and that rest and care *do* have an effect.
- Recognize that recovery from pain is a process, and that instant results are often short-lived and rarely permanent.
- Make certain that we are feeling actual pain, and that we are not, once again, making ourselves into victims of suffering.

• Instead of collapsing into helplessness, become available to help from the sources that have supported our recovery. We have not come this far only to get dumped now!

Until we have taken the first six Steps of the journey into recovery, it is very difficult—if not impossible—to attempt to use these measures. They are indicators of change, the effect of beginning a new way of living instead of relying on the old way of dying.

After we have taken Steps One through Six, we begin to gain a far deeper understanding of the magnitude of the gift of recovery we have been given. The gift has to be experienced, lived through, before we can become humble about receiving it.

And just as the experience of pain is itself very humbling, so is the release from pain. Many people in early recovery, including Dr. Bob, the co-founder of AA, went through days, weeks, months, and even years of living with the compulsion to use after putting down the drink or the drug! Some thought they could never endure it, but by using the tools of the program and the help they received, they survived. This period is a nightmare that can still evoke horrifying memories. None of us wishes to live through it again, and often the memory of it is what keeps our feet on the clean and sober path.

On this path, we are no longer victims, not because we no longer feel pain, but because we no longer suffer from the addiction to substances. The humiliation is over; humility in the face of recovery is ours to acknowledge. That is why Step Seven is placed in our way at this juncture on our journey. Unless we consciously become humble about our recovery, we are in significant danger of taking it for granted. "Victims will be victims," someone not very famous once said. We fall back easily into suffering, and in suffering we deprive ourselves of self-esteem.

Developing Self-esteem

The development of self-esteem is intimately linked with experiencing humility. Humility, not arrogance, is the key to adjusting the balance that has been missing in our lives. Most of us have lived at either one extreme of grandiosity or the other, either in triumph or in humiliation, either the brightest angel or the biggest slut. We have never known how to sustain ourselves in the middle ground. Step Seven, appearing in the middle of the Twelve Steps, proposes a basic idea that may never have occured to us: humility creates balance in life as we begin to rid ourselves of our obstacles.

Because it has taken a lifetime to acquire our secrets, our obstacles, our "defects of character," they are not simply going to vanish on their own overnight. We need to take some kind of consistent action in order to have them leave us. Looking back at our journey, we can observe that we have been working at the process: Step Four created an inventory and got our secrets out of hiding; Step Five shared them with another human being (along with a Higher Power); Step Six encouraged our willingness to have them removed; and now Step Seven suggests that we ask for help in dumping them. This is consistent action, if we link the four Steps together.

At the center of recovery is our willingness to deal with our obstacles, and each of the Twelve-Step programs focuses on this central activity in the ascent out of addiction.

Working on our own obstacles provides a consistent approach to achieving equilibrium in our lives. These obstacles are the survival tactics that have unbalanced us—in thought and action—and by working on them, we can make important changes that will influence our lives. Embodied in the Twelve Steps is the wisdom that self-renewal depends on the unusual combination of individual effort *and* asking for help from others, whether the group or the source of power beyond us. Personal effort, in these programs, does not mean recovering on one's own without outside assistance.

This is where humility enters. Because we cannot change entirely on our own, we need to learn to ask for help. For some of us, this is the most difficult effort of all. During our lives, most of us have been willing to give away many of our resources, sometimes without even having them. We learned to be people-pleasers instead of letting others know what they could have from us and what they couldn't. It was never possible, however, to tell them what it was *we* needed and what we didn't. When we were children, at a time when we needed to trust our parents, many of us were unable to do this because they told us that we did not know what we felt or thought. Their criticism established the rule "Don't trust!" This lies at the heart of our difficulty in receiving the love and support others may have wanted to give to us. Not trusting leads to isolation and feeling different. In recovery, working the Steps, we break down this isolation and establish communion with others.

We have already experienced, in Step Three, the effects of turning over our will and our lives to the care of God/HP as we understood God/HP. In Step Seven, we add our survival tactics and ask for help in getting rid of these obstacles standing in the way of our recovery. The willingness to ask for the help opens the way to a new freedom. Never have we asked for anything like this before. Operating always with the fear of being rejected, we usually tried to get what we wanted either by stealth or manipulation. Or, rather than be turned down, we did without. This effort of asking for help marks a milestone in our recovery.

In the past, if we did force ourselves to ask someone for something, it was often someone unable or unwilling to give it. This was one of the ways we, as victims, reinforced our lack of self-esteem and confirmed that the only way to survive in this world is by manipulation and dishonesty. When we can ask for what we need with the hope of receiving it, and from healthy people, we are saying that we are worthy. Whether or not they can give us what we ask, we raise our self-esteem and sense of self-worth.

The following are a few suggestions about implementing this Step:

- Remember that you need to be careful what you ask for. You might get it!
- Remember not to ask for something you don't really want.
- Remember that you are not making a deal, or manipulating in order to get your way. You are asking for what you need.
- Remember to be grateful for what you already have, for everything else will rest on this foundation.
- Remember that your words are important for you to hear in your own ears; you need to listen as you say them.
- Remember not to be ashamed to ask for anything that you truly need: if you're not ashamed to ask for it, HP won't feel ashamed to give it!
- Remember to be patient after you ask; things happen not in our time but in HP's time.

- Remember that the list of obstacles is usually quite long; ask for help in removing them one at a time instead of all at once. It is progress, not perfection, that makes the difference in recovery.
- Remember to ask for help with joy; children are sad only after they have been rejected—*not* before!
- Remember to say thanks!

Relating with Higher Power

I will never forget the rush of emotion I felt when I heard a man say that he *knew* he was a child of God, and that God loved him! I asked myself, "*If he knows that, why don't I?*" It took some time before I understood that what was preventing such a realization was all my guilt and shame over everything that had happened in my past. It was my first clue that my obstacles stood not only in the way of my future but also in the way of a different relationship with my Higher Power. It was essential for me to admit to myself that, as far as I knew, these obstacles made me unlovable.

Believing that because I am gay HP could love everyone except me had the effect of excluding God from my love—and my life. In canceling out HP from my life, I isolated myself from everyone and remained trapped in my own uniqueness. For me, this was the perfect precondition for spiritual bankruptcy.

One aspect of the depth and breadth of wisdom found in the Twelve Steps is the acknowledgment of a Higher Power not as conceived in our past—our childhood, or our addiction—but "as we understand" this power now, at this time. For many of us, it takes months and even years to leave behind our old ideas about God. This takes as long as it takes; it is left to each individual. Nevertheless, hanging on to old ideas keeps us stuck in the past; embracing new ones opens us to change.

Step Seven, "Humbly asked God to remove our shortcomings," is an active way of entering into a new and different relationship with a Higher Power. Some have referred to it as a "resting step," but it is actually a very active and pragmatic approach to dealing with what is optional in our lives: suffering.

Until we can understand that we are in charge of developing a relationship with HP different from that in the past, we will continue to suffer over the kind of relationship we have always had. Here is another paradox for us in recovery: by humbly asking for help to remove our shortcomings, we enter a new relationship with life that is based on help from a Higher Power and our worthiness to receive it. This goes far beyond identifying and acknowledging our obstacles. It is a giant step away from our past and into the present; it is change in its most basic form.

For many gay men and lesbians in recovery, it is a profound revelation to discover that God, or HP, loves them. This revelation is at the heart of the "spiritual awakening" referred to in the Twelve-Step programs. For many, I believe this awakening begins from the first day we hear the words "Keep coming back!" No one ever asked us to come back in our addiction—not even the drug dealers! (They knew we *had* to come back because we were hooked.) It is the caring and the unconditional love we have felt from others in recovery that has opened us to the possibility of trusting a power greater than our own.

Did we believe we were worth it when we were beginning our journey? Given the way we thought about ourselves, that does not seem likely. But a day at a time, we gradually came to believe that we were, indeed, worth it. Our choice kept us coming back, and coming back will continue to be our choice. We can take pride in this, because that is the part we have played: choosing sobriety instead of addiction. Parades and demonstrations for gay causes express support for our rights and our dignity as gay brothers and lesbian sisters; our sobriety celebrates, each day, our new lives as sober and free gay men and lesbians.

Recovery is something all of us do together, no matter what our belief or unbelief. The process of recovering has no time schedule, and there are as many ways as there are individuals who work at it. Of course, we can complain about this whenever we wish. We can also be humble about it. Like everyone else, we are human beings. Working on Step Seven, if we haven't already appreciated the slogan "God doesn't make garbage," we can now. We can also be grateful that we have the choice of taking these Steps on the journey into recovery.

GUIDES TO PROGRESS

"Me, arrogant? You must be kidding." Rick's face flushed as he pulled himself up in his chair.

"Hasn't anyone ever told you that before?" asked George, surprised at Rick's reaction.

"No one would ever have the nerve to accuse me of that. It's not true. Why just the other day. . ."

George interrupted him, "There you go again. You asked me for some feedback about why so many of the guys avoid going out to coffee with you now that you're sober. What do you do when I offer an answer? You start off in some other direction. Rick, you don't listen to what other people say; all you hear is yourself."

"And that's what you mean by 'arrogant'?" asked Rick.

"Well, if a man won't listen to what anybody else says, wouldn't you call him arrogant?"

Rick thought for a minute. "Do you have any suggestions about what I can do about it?" he asked.

"Sure. Start listening and stop talking," answered George.

"How will I know if it works?" asked Rick.

"You'll know." About a month later, George went by the window of the same coffee shop and saw Rick sitting at a table with six guys. Rick waved to him and winked. George's suggestion had been right on the money.

As far as Jane was concerned, she had done everything right. From the first day she began working on recovery by not picking up a drink or a drug, she had begun reading the Big Book, the book on the Steps, and everything else she could get her hands on. She could quote whole passages from the texts, but everyone—including her parents—acted toward her in exactly the same way as before. Why couldn't they see the change in her? After about eighteen months of loneliness and misery, she broke down and told her mother how terrible she felt. To her amazement, her mother embraced her for the first time in years and told her how good it was to discover that Jane actually needed help from someone else. "It's never to late to learn to be vulnerable. Believe me, it's not weakness but strength to let other people come into our lives," said Jane's mother. Being right was not the answer Jane thought it was; being available to help and support from others made all the difference in the world to her recovery.

Suggestions for Action

When you attend a meeting, listen to the words of others instead of comparing yourself with them. Don't compare your recovery with anyone else's, or even with your own from an earlier period. Whatever it takes to get and stay clean and sober is the prescription you need for your own recovery. You've got everything to support you in this task—if you choose to use it.

REFLECTIONS

We have never lost anything that we ever really had; we go on receiving what we need.

Step Eight

THE GIFT OF RESPONSIBILITY

CONDITION: IRRESPONSIBILITY

In addiction, we are caught in a quicksand of desperation in which one day is identical with the next, and the one after that. We slip deeper into despair and destruction. We are incapable of doing anything; we lose all sense of responsibility for our lives and for what happens to us.

ALTERNATIVE: RESPONSIBILITY

Most of the wreckage of the past is in human lives—our own and other people's. Owning our actions advances recovery because it involves being honest with ourselves about what change actually means. Real change means treating ourselves and others differently; setting the record straight is an important way to make this correction.

Accepting responsibility for our actions breaks down self-delusion and fantasy. We can now go on to be responsible for living a healthy and productive life in recovery instead of only reliving the past. "Look back, but don't stare!"

STEP EIGHT:

Made a list of all persons we had harmed, and became willing to make amends to them all.

Vivid images and fantasies from the past arise and flourish in our newly experienced recovery. These powerful impressions often disturb us as we attempt to make our way into new territory. "Somehow, no matter where I go, I always find that I bring myself with me." This strikes a familiar chord because we all have thought and acted in the past in ways that continue to affect us. No matter where we journey, we bring with us the memory of where we have been.

Extending the Focus

Up to this point, we have been working within the boundaries and limitations of our own thoughts and actions, and their impact on our lives. As unsure as we may have been in early recovery, we still felt safe enough because we kept the focus completely on ourselves without considering others. Even the person we chose as a sponsor, or to listen to our fifth Step, was someone we felt could help guarantee our safety. All this while, we have been tunneling through our personal histories to create the foundation for a clean and sober life. The time has come to extend the focus to include others.

It is natural to resist doing this. Our old pattern of isolating is always there waiting for us, and we recognize the temptation. Do we yield to it, or not? This is always our choice in sobriety. We live in today with our choices.

If we truly value this new life we have begun to live in recovery, there are choices we must make to support it. Valuing recovery means taking an active role in living it. This, then, *is* our new life; choosing recovery instead of addiction is entirely our own responsibility.

For some of us, the word *responsibility* is loaded with guilt over what we have failed to do with our lives, as well as blame for the mountains of things we have done. For many, introducing this word is the same as reminding them of old debts left unpaid that have accrued staggering interest. Alcoholics, in general, are not famous for taking responsibility for their lives, apart from securing the next drink. In recovery, this is one change we never thought it possible to make, and we make it with the loving support of others just like ourselves who we never believed were out there.

This is not the only change. Work is already in progress in another major area of concern: pain. In Step Seven, we identified some effective ways to handle pain, to play an active role in dealing with it. Wasn't this a different kind of role from the one we have been used to? In the past, we have never known what to do about pain. Our expertise has been in *suffering*. During our addiction, we assumed complete responsibility for living with suffering. Now, in recovery, we must begin to assume responsibility for getting rid of suffering. Acknowledging this shift in perspective is further progress in the process of recovery.

When we shed our status as life's victims, we no longer need to look out through eyes that search only for opportunities to suffer. How strange and different the world appears when we stop setting ourselves up for a life of suffering!

This may take us awhile, but gradually, we will begin to notice that, as gay men and lesbians, we have typically acted in ways that have ensured we would remain victims. We have invited others to prey on us and mistreat us. It may be very difficult to accept this realization. The most important thing, at this time, is that we understand we have played a key role. We need to understand that we have been active agents and not the passive pawns we are in the habit of pretending to be. We have not simply been "done to." We have, instead, consistently performed in ways that made it appear we had no responsibility for the disasters that always found us.

Recovery, at this stage in our journey, invites us to take an honest look at our role in relation to others. If we cannot see what we have done and the way we have done it, we are completely in the dark about changing. Observing these important patterns and events in our lives is the beginning of becoming responsible for ourselves.

In addiction, we made addictive choices; in sobriety, we can make sober choices. Acknowledging what our role has been in the past helps us to understand how we can begin to make different choices in the present. We do not change without seeing ourselves. The task always begins with us.

When we begin to understand how we have acted, the role we have played in provoking others to react in ways that ensured our victimization, we make a conscious connection with the source of power in our lives. If we have been able to make those others do as they have done, we understand that we can become responsible for doing what *we* now need to do for ourselves in order to recover! The role we have played in the past with other people provides us with important clues for today.

In Steps Four, Five, Six, and Seven, we initiated work on exploring the continents of our secrets, our mountain ranges of obstacles, our deserts of shortcomings. With Step Eight, we add to the map of our experience the names of the people we encountered along the way who are now an integral part of who we are in this moment. This Step introduces into our recovery everyone who has been with us in our lives before and during addiction.

Naming Names

Many of the disturbing fantasies that have intruded on our recovery have involved the people in our past: parents, brothers and sisters, other relatives, childhood playmates and grownup friends, husbands and wives and lovers, employers and strangers. The list goes on and on. Some of them are no longer living, but that doesn't matter. We keep all of them alive in our memories, and we reincarnate them and whatever they did or did not do to us every time we fantasize about them. They march like a parade of phantoms, always ready and willing to pass before our reviewing stand; they go in circles around us, and we go on and on experiencing what we did or didn't do with them. For some inexplicable reason, even in recovery, they seem to have some kind of special power over us, and we succumb to it whether or not we want to.

In the past, we felt unable to escape from our secrets or to stop using our survival tactics. We will never be able to do away with our fears of those who have this kind of power over our lives unless we now take the power away. These fears stand in the way of our recovery. Didn't we discover a new kind of freedom when we inventoried and faced our secrets? Now, we will find a different way to live with people from our past if we face our fears by bringing their names out of the shadows and into the light.

The actual process of developing a list might include the following steps:

- Begin by identifying situations in which you experience guilt and blame, both in addiction and in recovery.
- Recall as many of the participants in these situations as you can, and call them by name.
- Instead of hiding from them, write their names on the list.
- Let the feelings these names evoke come up within you.
- Allow these feelings to reverberate in your memory and connect with identical situations in which different people were involved.
- Write their names on the list.
- Don't attempt to write a complete list of names on the first day you begin.
- Put the list in a safe place; plan to look briefly at it each day during the period you are working the Step.
- Discuss the process of developing the list, and whatever it calls up for you, with your sponsor.
- *Do not consider taking any kind of action at this time.*

On the page, they are only names, but what memories they evoke! Summoning their names into the present, we often discover that our fears of these people have matured in our memory into a vintage brew of considerable proof! Over the years, guilt and shame have fermented the events we have experienced in the past into a concoction that may even taste strangely familiar, like something directly out of our addiction. Perhaps we are even sober enough to appreciate that we have used the fantasies about these people we have stored in our imagination in the same way we used alcohol or drugs—to get high or low over them.

Naming names is not an exercise in abstraction. When we name people from our past, the reverberations penetrate our mental, emotional and physical existence. We may find ourselves wishing to run and hide, but first we must show up with our reactions. Having come this far in our journey, we are aware that getting in touch with these feelings is crucial to our recovery.

We have denied our feelings about what we have done, or not done, to and with other people, just as we have denied the effects of the substances we abused in our addiction. In working Step Eight, we make a conscious effort to end this denial and admit the truth. In recovery, denial about anything or anyone stands in the way of progress.

We do not have to start from scratch; we can use the inventory we wrote in Step Four. Each of our secrets, each of our survival tactics, has involved other people. Not one of them is sealed away in a vacuum separated from human interaction. Unless we end our denial about this, we will go on watching that parade of phantoms circle in our imagination. This is the choice we must make: whether or not to call a halt to this kind of suffering.

Regretting the Past

Even in recovery, regret over the past is one of the surest ways to perpetuate it. Because of the efforts we have already made on our journey, we now understand that we can live in the present only when we become willing to face the past instead of hiding or running from it.

The shrill voice from a member of the committee inside our heads calls out to object: "That's all very well for you to say! You don't know what I've done to my mother/father/brother/sister/lover/spouse!"

Haven't we all done something to someone? Everyone shares this fate with everyone else, and no one is unique in this respect. Even though what each of us has done may be different, and there is, perhaps, some shred of uniqueness in the deeds themselves, nevertheless, they all have something in common: they have already been done; they are facts. Not one person can change anything that has already happened. In recovery, it helps to be very clear about this.

As strange as it may seem, people may understand this but refuse to think or act on their understanding. They persist in acting and thinking as if they can change what has happened in the past. For this reason, the past exerts a stranglehold over their lives. They do not live in today with today's *actual* opportunities but are throttled with yesterdays' and yesteryears' *lost* opportunities. Is it any wonder they live under a burden of suffering? Too many people take this burden of suffering for granted and allow it to destroy every opportunity they have for happiness.

We cannot do this if we are committed to progress on our journey into recovery. No matter what other people do with their lives, we need to learn to live without suffering. Many gay men and lesbians have a particularly difficult time accepting this and living it because of the distortions and lies they have allowed themselves to believe. Being gay does not mean living in the closet, or in a gay ghetto, or with hardship, misery, and failure. Gay men and lesbians have the same entitlements in life that everyone who is not gay has! We must claim them for ourselves. No one else can claim them for us.

This was not possible to do in our addiction, because drugs and alcohol controlled our lives. In recovery, we can begin to work at the task of claiming happiness, love, success and freedom for ourselves. Step Eight is crucial to providing the foundation for accomplishing this. Let us understand the reason.

In our lives before and during our addiction, we put on different disguises in front of other people. Not the least familiar of these disguises was the invisible "halo" of shame that some of us wore in front of heterosexuals. From the time we were children, perhaps, our sense of feeling different encouraged us to believe that something must be "wrong" with us, and therefore we had to deal with people in certain ways—some of them acceptable, others unacceptable. It is easy to understand that if something is "wrong" with us, then something must be "right" with other people. With this as the basis for our thinking and action, we have been responsible for giving away most of our power, because they are "right" and we are not. So many of the things we have done or not done in the past have been motivated by this mistaken conviction.

This is a basic premise for many of us. Another is, "If they are going to do *that* to me, then I'm going to do this to *them*." There is no doubt we have suffered (and we have caused others to suffer) by living this way. The wreckage of our past is the best evidence for what can happen to us when we do.

Most of this wreckage has been in human lives, our own and other people's. A woman I know calls the incidents themselves sins of commission, like stealing money from an employer or going to bed with our lover's best friend, and sins of omission, like not being there for others when they needed us, or failing to do what we have promised. These sins create a battlefield on which we will continue to suffer until we are willing to own our actions instead of grappling with our regrets.

Taking responsibility for what we have already done is real change. It is possible to treat ourselves and others differently from the way we have in the past. It marks a major departure from performing our familiar ritual of suffering over the way we have acted in the past. Taking this responsibility on ourselves gets us into the present.

With that, another voice from the committee in our head pipes up: "If that means I have no past, how is it then possible for me to have a future?" No one is suggesting that we can erase the past; everything that has happened has already happened. Regretting the past steals our energy; taking responsibility for our actions in the past restores it. We can see this in ourselves as we go about developing the list of names of those we have wronged over the years.

This list of names we make is for ourselves. At this place now in our journey, we can see only as far as our vision at this moment permits. Just as with all the other Steps, progress not perfection is the goal. The longer we are sober the more names we will remember. And there may be some we will never remember to put on this list. Our honest willingness to undertake this task is more important than any of the names we write, except one: our own.

At the Top of the List

Of all the people we have injured in our lives, we have harmed ourselves the most. The backlash of the harm we have done to others has devastated our own lives. We have deprived ourselves of the happiness that comes from healthy relationships and self-realization. We have wasted our gifts and lost touch with our value as feeling, thinking, loving human beings. We have put ourselves through the hell of addiction. No matter what anyone else has done to us, we have harmed ourselves more. Taking responsibility for this is an enormous step!

It takes many of us a long time to be able to understand this because of our deep-rooted sense of worthlessness and our lack of self-esteem. Our addiction has intensified all the feelings of inadequacy, incompetence, guilt and shame we have known as gay men and lesbians. No matter how low we have ever been before, alcohol and drugs have brought us lower. It is only through constant and loving encouragement that we can restore balance in our lives. We need to take each opportunity to acknowledge ourselves that a Twelve-Step program provides. Therefore, in working Step Eight, we need to place our own name at the top of the list of the people we have harmed.

Taking this initiative for the first time, perhaps, we make a list of the names of those who have waved the banners of our darkest secrets as they marched through our imagination in our phantom parades. Mother, father, brothers, sisters, husbands, wives, lovers, children, friends, enemies, employers, employees, friends, strangers—the Step encourages us to name as many as we can remember.

Often when we do this, something unusual happens, and it is important to note it here. There is now a difference when these people we have harmed appear before our imagination. *We* have summoned them; they have not sprung out at us from nowhere, the way they usually do! By writing their names, we introduce a new element into any relationship we ever had with them. This may be the first inkling of what taking responsibility for ourselves means, being a gay and sober son, a lesbian and sober daugther, and so on, in relationship with anyone, whoever he or she is, was, or might have been.

Many of our relationships in the past have been completely out of balance. Our secrets, our dishonesty, our lack of trust for other people, have affected us deeply whenever we tried to connect. We ourselves have suffered over what we attempted to hide, as well as from the dishonest relationships that resulted from these efforts. The others have suffered too. Dishonesty and duplicity have diminished us. We have not been the person we appeared to be. How many times have we used this as the reason for drinking or using?

Step Eight is not about fault or blame. This Step is another opportunity to examine the survival tactics we developed that, by now, have become obstacles. By identifying the events of our past, we are acknowledging the role we have played in them. About one thing, we should be very clear. Believing it is possible to hide from any of those we have harmed is as threatening to our recovery as attempting to hide from our secrets. It protects us against change; it supports the addictive pattern of denial. If we can believe this instead, we will be able to overcome our natural reluctance to rake up old memories and will concentrate our efforts on this task.

Many of us, in this Step, encounter a deep sense of sorrow the moment we begin to work on it. How badly we have disappointed those we have loved and who have loved us! How cruelly we have rewarded those who have been kind to us! Perhaps we could not see it in the past, but we can certainly see it now. We must remind ourselves that when our blindness is ended, the very least we can do is be grateful for the light. Restoration of our ability to feel gratitude is one of the changes that occurs in recovery. We can accept it with joy instead of sorrow.

The people from our past provide us with a rich reservoir of images and memories in much the same way as our addiction provided us with a rich source of fantasies. We can give ourselves the space in which to change by putting the past in its proper place. With all our thoughts and feelings loaded with the past, we have no room either to live in the present or to change in the future. When we understand this, that "responsibility" means we must take action to separate what was from what is, we change our concept of it.

Taking Responsibility for Recovery

We are constantly using our energy at cross-purposes when we insist on the past functioning in our lives as if it were the present. The act of separating is an act of responsibility. It defines, "This is mine *now*" and "That was mine *then*." Getting into the present means identifying what is past and using our energy to handle, in whatever way we can, the business of today. Appreciating our possibilities for action, along with our limitations, establishes balance in our lives. We become clear in our own minds about what it is possible to do about the past as we begin to exercise this responsibility.

When memories and fantasies confuse what we can do with what we cannot do, we have no opportunity to act. Even in recovery, we can become so caught up in all the things we haven't been able to do, or have left undone, that we become paralyzed, unable to do anything. We create balance in the present with our attitudes about what we *can* do and what we *cannot* do. Staying stuck in our fantasies about and from the past (as well as the present) keeps us off balance.

A Step at a time, we have been learning how to take responsibility for our recovery. Living in the present, we assume an active role of creating balance that is completely different from our previous role of seeking escape. The process began with Step One, and Step Eight follows the natural progression.

Now, we are no longer helpless; we are no longer victims; we are no longer lost to our addiction. The choice we have been given in sobriety is no longer to wear any of the disguises we have worn in the past. Acknowledging who we have been and who we are now marks an end to irresponsibility.

As essential to this Step as writing our list of names is our willingness to make amends for our actions. Changing from the way we have been in the past takes more than a writing excercise. The person we have been has caused harm; accepting responsibility begins with the willingness to do what we can to make amends to alleviate that harm. Willingness, for many of us, may take considerable time to develop; nevertheless, we need to make this effort because it provides us with a solid basis on which to create our lives in recovery.

We are no longer going to live in isolation, and we are no longer going to treat people the way we have treated them in our addiction. Step Eight provides us with a "declaration of independence" from the irresponsible gay man or lesbian we have been. It gives us the opportunity to act responsibly with everyone on our list as well as every new person who comes into our lives in sobriety. We extend the boundaries and limitations of our world as we become more able and willing to exercise this freedom.

With this gift of responsibility we have given ourselves, we can work on living a healthy and productive life in recovery instead of only reliving the past. That means we can no longer allow the past or anyone from the past to control our lives. In Step Eight, we make our first claim to being who we are now, and we allow the people whose names we have written on our list to emerge from our imagination and stand on their own. Living in the present depends on this.

GUIDES TO PROGRESS

Fran had been writing letters to her sons for the past year without any response. They were old enough to write back. Why hadn't they written? Over the weekend she called them, and though they said they were glad to hear her voice, they still sounded strange. It was as though an enormous wall had built up between them. She kept thinking about this, and the more she thought, the emptier she felt inside. She found herself in tears several times a day, and at night she cried herself to sleep. When she called Marci, a lesbian in her building who sometimes went to meetings with her, Marci could hardly understand her on the telephone.

"Are you sober, Fran?" Marci asked.

"Yes, I feel like drinking, but I haven't done it," Fran answered. Marci came right over.

When Marci got there, Fran told her everything that had happened over the years since her separation and divorce from her husband, who was still an active alcoholic. Then she told her about sharing the truth of being a lesbian with her teenage sons. "I hear everything you've told me, Fran, and you know something? It's all ancient history. Now tell me what's happened since you called them on the weekend." Marci asked.

"Nothing has happened; I just feel terrible, that's all."

"The fact is, you called them; they spoke to you; and four days have passed since then, right?"

"Yes, that's right," Fran answered.

"Well, your feelings are important. They're who you are—today. But they're not facts! Later, or tomorrow, they can change. Just like your sons' feelings can change. You can only be responsible for your own feelings, not for theirs. If you take care of yourself, the way you've learned over the past year in the program, your feelings *will* change."

"Are you sure?" asked Fran.

"Feelings aren't facts; you can count on them to change! Put a nice cool cloth on your eyes, and then we'll go out to the deli for a corned beef sandwich. I'll bet you haven't eaten much today, have you?"

"No, I haven't," Fran answered.

"*Hungry* is the first letter of HALT, remember. We'll look at *Angry*, *Lonely*, and *Tired* after we've tackled that one." Two years have passed, and Fran is still working through her relationship with her sons; one of them spent Christmas with her last year. That night she talked her heart out to Marci she would never have believed such a visit was possible.

Peter had not been able to stay clean and sober for longer than six months. Six months was his milestone, and this time he had done it—with the help of lots of friends in the program and a sponsor who spent a great deal of time with him. It was only after his sponsor had left for a Roundup that Peter realized he was on his own for the first weekend in his sobriety. Drink signals started coming up for him. He felt afraid and nervous. He called Bill, and they talked about it. The feeling went away.

"Just look at the evidence, Pete. You're eight months sober, you've got your health and your job back, you've got lots of support whenever you need it. What's that line I've heard you say? 'I'll be fine, as long as I remember that I'll be fine.' Let me hear you say it." Peter said it and got through another day sober.

Suggestions for Action

We need to learn to own our feelings instead of stuffing them; calling them by name is the beginning of allowing ourselves to have them. The next time you are anxious or upset, stop and think a moment. What is the name of the feeling? "Angry?" "Disappointed?" "Afraid?" Perhaps you have several feelings at the same time. Observe what happens when you sort them out. We cannot begin to work at changing any of our feelings until we have identified them.

REFLECTIONS

The world that surrounds us is not a neat, orderly, or loving world. And yet, the forces that encourage order and love are there if we will choose them.

Step Nine

FUSING THE FRAGMENTS

CONDITION: SUFFERING AND FRAGMENTATION

When we were addicts, our lives collapsed into smaller and smaller pieces. Even the tiniest decisions terrified us. Fragmentation resulted from the growing inability to reverse this ever-worsening slide; irresponsibility and disorder accelerated. No matter what we did to try to cope with the situation, we could not explain why we were falling apart. We suffered over everything.

ALTERNATIVE: HEALING AND FUSION

Owning our actions in the past reverses our direction. Making amends to others is as cleansing and healing an activity as Step Five—as long as we are clear about the need to do it for *ourselves*. When we remove the debris from relationships, we find it possible to make room for different, better, healthier relationships now and in the future.

Forgiving ourselves accelerates when others we have wronged forgive us. Whether they do or not, we have made the effort and have taken responsibility for our lives. Doing this fuses the fragments together into a new configuration in which to live a new life.

STEP NINE:

Made direct amends to such people wherever possible, except when to do so would injure them or others.

Living in the present is different from what we think it will be. As we work the Steps, an orderly routine begins to emerge out of the chaos of our unmanageable lives. Now, we wake up, we get washed, we have breakfast, we wash the dishes, we read some program literature, we go to work, we go to a meeting, and so on into the day. As the months continue, we find the opportunity, in the space created by our routine, to make some important connections with the past. These connections help us begin to live in a new way.

"More shall be revealed." All of the Twelve-Step programs stress the effect of time on recovery. No matter what we understand today, each day that follows provides the opportunity to understand even more about ourselves. It took me several years into my own routine before I made a connection—crucial for my own recovery—with a pivotal incident from my childhood. Writing about it, I can still feel what it was like being back there in the body of the three-year-old who actually had the experience.

His Story

Standing at the top and looking down, he stared at the flight of stairs before him and hesitated. They seemed too long and too steep for him ever to make it to the bottom. His small hand reached up to touch the bannister above his head for support. It was smooth and firm.

He had been wakened from a nap, and dressed in short, white starched pants and a white starched shirt with buttons on it. His feet felt odd in the new shoes, which pinched. From the living room below, he could hear strange voices. The sound frightened him, although he didn't know why. He could remember nothing from before his nap, neither his excitement at the arrival of the guests who were coming to celebrate Thanksgiving at his house nor any of the pleasure he had felt doing the little tasks he'd been given in the preparations. At this moment, all he felt was terrifying anxiety, as if he were coming apart in many pieces.

His mother touched his shoulder, and he began his descent. The pitch of the voices grew louder and louder. His progress slowed; his three-year-old legs did not want to bend. With each step, the feeling grew larger and larger within him—if only he could become *invisible!* Then, as he reached the bottom, completely surrounded by a circle of faces high above him, he suddenly burst into tears. "That's how he is sometimes," he heard his mother say behind him. From behind her explanation, he felt a part of himself actually become invisible.

Remembering this incident from my past connected me with the place I had started from: it revealed to me the moment when I had first wished to be invisible. Without ever realizing it, I made this moment the basis for the way I interacted with other people from then on.

Over these last years of my journey in recovery, I have spent a great deal of time getting in touch with that little boy inside me. Because of the willingness to face the way I have lived during my lifetime and my responsibility for relating with others, amazing things have happened. This process has meant lots of space-clearing, mind-uncluttering, and letting go, and, at the same time, making the consistent effort to live in the present. I have been able to make new and different connections with the things I know and understand, and these insights have helped me to care about myself and others in new ways. As I have made the journey, what has become most clear to me is that the Twelve Steps are about becoming an adult instead of continuing to live as a child or an adolescent. Perhaps the key I have found is that in order to grow up, I need to show up in my life.

The three-year-old descending the staircase refused to enter that people-filled room because it meant revealing how different from them he felt. That was the last thing he wanted to do! Because he desperately wished to fit in, to be a member of the family, he chose invisibility instead. He held back a dimension of himself from everyone else, and this is how the pattern began of never being "all there" for anyone—not even himself! Whatever caused that three-year-old's initial response to others, his orientation to the world was so deeply affected that he was unable to live in it any other way except "invisibly."

The Invisible Person

Some gay men and lesbians have chosen invisible lives rather than be exposed to rejection, punishment, abandonment—or worse. Others may have chosen very visible roles as heroes, or clowns, or mascots, while still others became scapegoats or rebels. All have experienced a great deal of suffering and despair in these roles. How many times have we used alcohol or drugs to isolate ourselves and bury the feelings that kept coming up because we were hiding who we really were? Let's be certain about this: we did not choose any of these roles because of our honesty. We isolated ourselves to keep other people from knowing how guilty we felt and to protect our dishonesty.

The effect was fragmentation. We broke ourselves up into hundreds of thousands of pieces that neither "all the king's horses and all the king's men" *nor addiction* could put back together again. No matter what the occasion, there were always certain "invisible" pieces of our lives that appeared at the most unexpected moments. These never fit in with the rest of the puzzle. It was impossible to get the whole thing to work together. Dishonesty consistently shielded some of the parts while it exaggerated or minimized at different moments the importance of other fragments. We could never be "all there" because there were just too many vanishing pieces to be there with. Our daily lives have been infinitely more complicated by the need to keep our sexual orientation invisible.

But perhaps this claim I've just made sounds unwarranted. If it does, then remember the periodic interrogations by parents about the people we were dating and when they could meet these prospective sons-in-law or daughters-in-law. Remember the constant pressure we felt to be on guard in conversation with them and others, changing the personal pronoun from *he* to *she*, or vice versa, and the fear of getting caught by a brother or a sister, or some other relative, with a friend who was so obviously gay we'd never be able to explain it. If this ever happened (and it inevitably did), remember the endless questions that never failed to come up each time we met whoever had "caught" us. Perhaps some of us were even married and then met someone of our own sex—and fell head over heels in love for the first time. Remember the confusion and despair we felt as well as created?

Living invisible lives creates devastating bad faith, which influences every relationship we have. In addition to the havoc this wreaks on other people's lives, it utterly fragments our own! No matter how long we get away with it, actually succeed in deceiving others, our own self-esteem is eaten away by the mistrust we naturally begin to feel for ourselves. Because we know the truth, we can never get away with the lie to ourselves. We spawn repulsive monsters—at least as large as the ones we were told stories about as children—in the realms of deceit in which our invisible selves hide their being.

We never escape from these monsters. Unless we not only become willing to face them, but then actually follow through, they will always be there to torture us. The process of becoming willing to do this takes time, patience, courage and the wish to continue on the journey of recovery. We need to consistently remind ourselves of this wish if we are going to work at changing our old rules for living.

For years, we have lived with rules that allowed us to preserve our invisibility by manipulating facts, events, and other people in ways we believed would assure we would get what we needed. We became experts at manipulation. Victims are always experts at manipulation. It should come as no surprise when along our journey into recovery, we try to use the old rules in this new life we are beginning. Perhaps other people have pointed this out, and that observation has startled us. How lucky we are now to have friends who care enough about us to tell us things like this!

Nevertheless, we do not change because we know better. The truth is for most of our lives we have known much better than we have ever done. Now, in recovery, the issue is, What will we do about it? Each of the Steps is an action step, and we need to take the action they suggest if we are to progress on the journey.

Careful thought has certainly been required, and with it we developed the basic inventories in Steps Four and Eight. But we did not write these lists to bury them in a drawer. We wrote them in order to begin to act differently. To accomplish this, we must get rid of some of our old rules, and one of the basic ones relates to the manner in which we deal with others.

Creating a Sober History

The willingness to change our old rules is essential even if we do not understand what new rules might be. When we first began our journey with Step One, few if any of us started out with very much understanding - (let alone intention) - of becoming responsible for our lives. All that most of us wanted to do was to stop the pain and suffering of addiction and surrender our claim to managing the mess our lives had become. No one said anything about responsibility. No one said anything, either, about manipulation. Our willingness to follow the directions suggested in the Steps has lead us into territory some of us never considered worth the time or the effort. "How did I ever end up here?"

In recovery, we direct our attention to the way we have lived previously in order to change how we will live now and in the future. Many people in Twelve-Step programs choose to go on living in the story of their addiction instead of becoming willing to create a clean and sober history for themselves in recovery. We hear them go on and on in meetings about people, places, and things that are long gone. They live in their stories about them today as if it *were* yesterday. The miracle is that we are alive today *in spite of* our stories; we need to remember this.

From the moment we start to work on Step One, even though we do not understand why we have been given this chance, we begin to to create a sober history; we add to this account each day we use our energy to work the program of recovery. Showing up in our lives as the person we are now instead of the person we have been in the past, we own what we have done. We recognize that denying it is the surest way of finding ourselves back in addiction.

A step at a time, we have gone about reclaiming our lives for ourselves. New understanding of ourselves has come with patience and willingness; we do not suddenly find ourselves "struck" responsible! Our journey prepares us as we go. Gradually, we discover a major difference in ourselves. Instead of focusing on what other people have done, we begin looking at *our* role in whatever has happened in our lives. Along with what we see about ourselves, we also become aware that the importance of recovery, in which we are no longer victims but the source of change, has shifted many of our priorities. In Step Nine, the time has come for us to live through with others the experience of being who we are now, instead of who we have been in the past.

Recovery programs have helped us to see that we cannot be rescued from life. Exactly as life is, and exactly as we are, we have learned that in sobriety we have the opportunity to live through our experiences. This does not mean merely to suffer through and survive them, for that is closer to "dying through" than living through. *Living through* (experiencing every moment of our existence coming at us via the feelings, emotions or happenings we are conscious of) means that we have the ability to be the man or the woman we are—

to show up with our own strength and weakness, our own power, and our own vulnerability—instead of being invisible. Showing up in our lives and *living through* them, experiencing an authentic relationship with everthing and everyone in the world, especially ourselves, is a vital affirmation that supports our recovery.

Each Step has encouraged us to act in a new way instead of continuing in the old ways with the old rules. Step Eight began the process of going beyond ourselves to consider our relationships with others. No matter what we may have done in the past, we were encouraged to become willing to make amends to the people we have harmed. This is a major change for us. In our addiction, if and when we ever said we were sorry about anything we had done to someone, it was usually because we wanted something. In our recovery, when we make amends to parents, family members, friends, lovers, it is because we understand that our lives as clean and sober people depend on it.

Showing up for ourselves makes it possible for us to live through who we really are, as well as providing us with the sober experience of who others really are. For many of us, this experience is a first. Whether other people in our lives accept it or not, we are inviting everyone to show up. When we arrive here in this new space together, we can begin to learn about emotional intimacy. In our new honesty, in learning to talk about how we really feel, about who we really are, our fears, our hopes, sadness and joy, we become authentic. Coming home to ourselves with authenticity makes us whole.

The fragmentation we created because of our need to hide from others reached its furthest limits in our addiction. In contrast, every effort we have been making to recover has been centered on developing wholeness, a core of identity, that can be known by everyone and nurtured with honesty and self-esteem. Invisibility supports neither. We are aware that we no longer need deceit and invisibility for protection, because we are developing a new way to live by working the Steps.

Fear, Guilt, and Resentment

Throughout most of our life, the fear and guilt that being gay men or lesbians created in us has been the basis for the way we have related with other people. If we examine the inventory we wrote in Step Eight, we will be startled to count how many people on our list have been harmed not because we intended it but because of this source of fear and guilt. Whether they were straight or gay, our interactions with them were often influenced by the protection we sought in invisibility. Terrified of ever being totally ourselves, we have said and done things that cheated both them and us of authenticity. When we cheat others, we must always suffer an inner loss of some kind.

Along with losing other people's trust, we have lost our own self-esteem as well as our own power to create happiness and satisfaction in our lives. In our fear and guilt, we have given away to others the power to approve of us or to deny us approval. We have become people-pleasers, manipulators, victims and escape artists. Much of the harm we have done has been in wearing these disguises. It is mind-boggling to realize that all we really have to do to change is get in touch with our feelings and trust those we love enough to talk with them about these feelings!

Instead of continuing to live invisibly or behind disguises, we need to live through the experience of acknowledging the roles we have played in the lives of the people whose names we have written on our list. Journeying further into recovery means that we face them with our honesty and accept responsibility for our actions, because that is how we restore our self-esteem and our power to live our lives completely and spontaneously.

In taking Step Nine, we have to find words that seem right to us. There is no formula for making amends. Face to face, on the telephone, in letters, some people go into great detail about what they have done during their addiction. Others keep it as simple as possible and say, "I'm sorry." Many have written letters to people who are no longer alive; sometimes they read these to a sponsor and then burn them. We need to do what fits us in recovery and allow ourselves to make mistakes. It is surprising how we seem to "accidentally" meet people to make amends to once we have become willing to do this!

I've had many different experiences in making amends; people's responses run the gamut: "I never thought you'd have the courage." "You must have been a very unhappy person." "It seemed as if you were oblivious to anyone except yourself." "Wow! I've never met anyone before who would take responsibility for something he could have got away with." "It sounds to me as if you've been through hell and back." "What a shock! So much is explained, now that I know. Thank you." "I never understood you before, and I don't understand you now!" "It's too late; but I'm glad you told me." "I'm glad you finally found out who you are. Keep it up!" "Listen, I never want to see you again, and no matter what you say, I'll never forgive you."

Not everyone we make amends to can accept them. Some of the people we have harmed are unwilling to let go of the deep resentment they feel over the way we have treated them. There is nothing we can do about that but accept it. The new rules we are learning to live with in recovery no longer include fixing other people. Their resentments belong to them, and we must allow those who choose resentments to have them.

What is important for us to be aware of is that the control these people have had over our lives is rooted in the power we give them. They have used it like a club over us, and it is not surprising that they are unwilling to loosen their grip. That we will no longer be victims is a loss certain people do not easily accept. We threaten the precarious balance of every unhealthy relationship when we insist on getting well.

Unfortunately, before, as well as during, our addiction, we have been in relationships with some people we would not have chosen had we been healthier. In addition to these people, many of us have families deeply affected by the alcoholic or otherwise dysfunctional environments in which we grew up as children or lived as adults. The disease has affected every family member because alcoholism is a family disease. Many of these family members are still drinking and using, and that is their choice. Nevertheless, we can still make amends to them for what *we* have done and go on from there.

Our recovery depends on the efforts we are willing to make to get rid of our resentments, and there is nothing that supports resentment like guilt and shame. Clearing out the wreckage of our past can only be accomplished through:

- being willing to deal with these resentments;
- accepting responsibility for what we have done to create them;
- taking action to acknowledge our responsibility by making amends to those we have harmed.

We are prisoners of the harm we have done to others, and we have harmed ourselves by it. When we ask them to forgive us for what we have done to them in our addiction, we release ourselves from the prison in which we have lived.

It is not a risk many of us have ever considered taking. What if they refuse even to talk to us, let alone forgive us? Is this some kind of religious ritual that everyone has to undergo in order to belong to a Twelve-Step program? What about the advice we've been given: "What anybody else thinks of me is none of my business"? The resistance to taking this Step takes many forms, and people in recovery frequently balk at it. There is no turning back from it, however, because we change our rules for living by actually living in a different way than we did in the past! Where we used to run from confrontations, where we buried or numbed our feelings with alcohol and other drugs, now we deal with life head-on and discover we will be OK.

By putting ourselves at the top of the list, which I suggested as a way to begin our inventories in Step Eight, we can gain some valuable experience when we begin work on Step Nine. Forgiving ourselves is a process that goes to the heart of recovery, because *we* know, perhaps better than anyone else, all that we did to wreck our lives in the past. To begin to forgive ourselves for this, to be willing to give up the shame and guilt we have stockpiled over the years of our addiction, to face ourselves with the facts instead of the fantasies is a momentous task.

This Step also takes a great deal of time. It is not possible to complete in a week, or a month, or a year. We find ourselves remembering more and more about the past and the people who lived it with us as we continue our journey in recovery. Over the years, no matter how long it takes, we discover that there is no one who can rescue us from the work that must be done on the obstacles that fear, shame, and guilt create in our lives. The only way forward is to *live through* them—to "show up" and experience ourselves as we are, as we have become, and to let each moment in our lives be positive instead of a source of punishment and harm for ourselves. We learn to love ourselves as we are when we forgive ourselves our past.

One of the most precious things I have learned is that when I confront the obstacle, whatever or whoever it is, I do not collapse. Instead of my worst scenarios, usually something far better than I ever expected occurs. This experience has had a major impact on changing the way I relate as an adult with everyone. The little boy descending the staircase, who was certain he was going to come apart when he confronted the world, discovered through Step Nine that invisibility was no longer a better alternative than showing up.

All of us have told ourselves many things about the way we must live as gay men and lesbians. We have been afraid of doing and not doing at the same time. We have been afraid of others and loved them at the same time. We have been afraid to discover, to reach out, to be who we wish to be, and at the same time, we have discovered and reached out. But we have not been the person we wished to be; we have been afraid to live, and still gone on living.

We have invited and allowed fears engendered by others as well as ourselves. Many of these have had to do with images and ideas of ourselves as "me" and "not me": "Oh, I can't do that; it's not me!" It is easier to live in imagination than risk the real test: "I'd rather not know what they want than to have to deal with the truth!" The list of fearful things we told ourselves is endless, and many of us may even be afraid of living *without* those fears! In sobriety, we have the opportunity to change our rules and confront these fears. The test of our ability comes when we face first ourselves and then other people, and push right on through the fears we have that we are *not* OK and *not* forgivable.

Showing Up in Our Lives

Instead of escaping as we have done in the past, we now have the chance to become an active participant instead of an invisible player. The dreadful anxiety we have endured over what the people we have wronged will do when we make amends to them vanishes when we actually do it. We *live through* it, and each time we do, our self-esteem increases. In having the courage to ask for forgiveness, whether or not it is granted, we have taken the action that living responsibly requires. We have shown up in our lives, and now, head to head with other people, we have the possibility of honest interaction with them.

No one else can do this for us. Through our efforts to make amends, we fuse the fragmentation that has always dispersed our lives. Having *lived through* the encounters with people and relationships that have been riddled with survival behavior, we can begin to experience healthy responses to other people. Step Nine presents us with the opportunity to gain insights through action. We all need these insights in order to enter into a different relationship with our lives.

I have known many people who have worked on this Step early in recovery. It brings them great relief to confront the way they dealt with people in the past because it clears the way for them to change how they will behave in the future. Nevertheless, we should not rush into other people's lives with our amends. The hurt we have brought to some of them is very deep, and our own healing process from our addiction must be far enough along to support us through the confrontation. Remembering that we choose to take this Step not for them but for ourselves, we do not expect more than they can give. And whatever they can give will have to be enough. Forgiveness is a gift that healthy people can grant freely because it belongs entirely to them. It allows them to get on with the business of their lives, but they must discover this for themselves. For those who offer it, the healing forgiveness brings will help them begin to put the pieces of their own lives back together again.

The act itself helps us to make amends to ourselves by celebrating a new way to live responsibly with the people who have been in our lives, the people from whom we have hidden through our invisibility, denial and dishonesty. In recovery, we are entitled to our place at the family table of the human race, and we need to claim it.

GUIDES TO PROGRESS

Stan's face was twisted, and it was all he could do to continue sitting in the chair instead of flinging himself out the door of his counselor's office. He had been sober for a year and a half, and because of the beneficial effect this had on his heart, he had gradually reduced the dose of Valium the doctor had prescribed. For a month, he had been completely off the drug. His withdrawal was even more difficult than from alcohol, and he had started seeing a counselor. That day had been a particularly tough one. His new boss had started making jokes about "sissies," and "those boys in the band." Stan was upset by it. "Damn it! I want to feel good!" he said through his clenched teeth.

"Listen, ninny! you *feel*, and that's good!" answered his counselor.

A smile flooded Stan's face as he said, "You know, you're right!"

Her heart was pounding, her mouth felt dry, and her thoughts were racing. Brenda had thought that all the anger and hurt she felt about her old lover, Pat, had been left far behind. She had changed jobs, moved to a different city, started working on her recovery from speed and booze, and as far as she knew, their old life together was a thing of the past. An hour before, she had seen Pat downtown with another woman, and all her old feelings had welled up again. She felt as if she were back at square one instead of ten months clean and sober. Suddenly, she remembered the second Step. Her life with Pat had been really *insane*; was that what she wanted back again? No way! She knew she had a lot more invested in this new way of living than to throw it all away on something that hadn't worked in the past. No, she wasn't back at square one. But yes, she realized, she had lots of work to do on her denial about her feelings for a woman she had blotted out of her consciousness.

Suggestions for Action

For such a long time, we lived either "high" or "low" on substances. Those feelings became natural to us. Learning to love something in the middle, neither "high" nor "low," takes getting used to.

Instead of sabotaging our efforts, we can begin to value balance by calling every day we do not use drugs or alcohol a "good" day. We need to write these words in our journal: "I had a good day today." Seeing this affirmation is the beginning of a pattern of support we will continue to develop throughout recovery. Good days add up to better and better ones, if we'll let them.

REFLECTIONS

When we begin to know ourselves, we also begin to know the Higher Power in us. What we know brings us closer to the higher; what we hide keeps us apart from this influence in our lives.

THE WAY OUT OF CROSS-PURPOSES

CONDITION: BACKSLIDING

The fragmentation in the day-to-day lives of addicts is the effect of cross-purposes on their own inner life. Multitalented, alcoholics disperse their energy in the cross-purposes that bombard them. This continues even in recovery. Addiction stymies performance; in recovery, energy is restored, and once again they are at the mercy of their many talents.

ALTERNATIVE: SELF-DISCIPLINE

Staying close to the mirror of observation, we come to understand ourselves through what we actually do day by day and not what we wish to do in our imagination. Slipping into delusion is easy after a lifetime of doing it; staying in reality takes vigilance and daily effort. Establishing priorities for action follows the effort at taking inventory. We need to "keep it simple" no matter how far along we are in the recovery process.

STEP TEN:

Continued to take personal inventory and when we were wrong promptly admitted it.

Did any of us believe we would come this far in our journey into recovery? Not that we haven't been in many unusual or complicated places before in our lives as gay men and lesbians. But this is the first time we find ourselves so much more a part of, instead of apart from, the place we live in and the people we live with. Now, as active participants in the day-by-day events that once bored or frightened us, we have stepped out of our fantasies, shared our secrets, and allowed ourselves our feelings instead of living only in our thoughts. We have observed the process at work and the effort that is required of us to make changes. What this has meant is that, clean and sober, we show up exactly as we are in our lives instead of wearing any disguises. Now, we can work at connecting our feelings with our thoughts instead of living as if their divorce was as much a part of our recovery as it was of our addiction.

Becoming Part Of

Identifying the obstacles to recovery within ourselves as well as those outside ourselves has been very important. It is only when we have done this that we can begin to use our energy directly on the task of working through our problems instead of obsessively holding onto the obstacles. Old patterns have, nevertheless, stuck with us. We have felt quite confused about how to live clean and sober lives, not to mention how uncertain and vulnerable we still feel without the support of the substances we used for escape. Any one or all of these obstacles may get in the way and alarm us enough to wonder if we have made any progress at all in our recovery.

It may seem like a long time ago that we set out on the journey. We may have begun to take for granted finding ourselves in today, alive and sober. This may even have provoked in us an occasional response of, "So what?" It is strange how so many of those "terrible" and "wonderful" things we did in our addiction may now seem much less terrible or wonderful. Our perspective has definitely shifted away from such dramatic contrasts, for we no longer need to constantly create them on our own. None of this has been easy, but we now consider all that "old stuff" behind us. "Is there something more?" we ask.

Once we passed through the ordeal of withdrawal, our bodies responded with amazing changes that we have come to accept as natural. Since then, our minds have begun clearing, slowly but surely. We can now remember where we parked the car, if we still have a car, and whether or not we ate or slept the night before. We no longer open our eyes in the morning to find ourselves in strange beds with people we have never seen before. "Is there something *more*?"

One important discovery we have made about our new lives is that as gay men and lesbians we are a part of, instead of separate from, the human race, that we contribute to it every time we make the effort—either as participants or only witnesses to what happens. Witnessing life is as essential as an audience is to a performance in the theater. Every one of us is necessary. We have been invited to life, and the celebration is going on all the time. We understand that we are welcome members of the troupe, the assemblage—the family. *That's* the meaning of the precious invitation we have accepted in sobriety.

Along with this invitation has come the opportunity to enjoy life, to find happiness as we discover ourselves in it. We do this by sharing ourselves with others. Sharing what we feel and understand with others is something we have learned, with practice and support, that we *can* do. The Twelve-Step programs have provided us with the unusual opportunity to be a friend, a fellow recoverer, a sponsee or sponsor, and a witness to others who know nothing more than that they are suffering the calamity of addiction. When we choose to share our gift, it becomes an act of recovery.

The Attitude of Gratitude

Most of the people I have met on my journey have felt deeply grateful at being given another chance at life. Years ago, as a child who was very poor in math, I remember being told, "You're going to do it until you get it right." At the time, that was a punishment. Getting it right, now, means something different from what I thought it meant. It's about living life without alcohol and drugs—clean and sober. As bewildering as it seems, all of us have been given this chance in recovery, and we need to learn that just being alive means we deserve this chance. As we learn to love ourselves more each day, we come to realize without reservation that we deserve the best!

Gratitude can open the way to wonder. We may be filled with wonder about everything and everyone each day of our lives. Life in sobriety is amazing. The feast it provides is always filled with surprises, from hearing prayers we never thought would come from our mouths in the morning to closing our eyes without pain at night. All too many of us had never known what some of the basic experiences in life were like—sex, for example—unless we used drugs or alcohol. What we did, who we did it with, whether or not we enjoyed it was more or less a blur. For those who may need some reassurance, sex is a glorious new discovery in recovery! Now, it can fill us with wonder for the first time.

Isn't it amazing that almost nothing is the way we have planned? Usually, it's much better. We are filled with spontaneity instead of the deadening desire to manipulate to a particular result. We are able to decide what we wish to do each day and to know we will not arrive drunk or "high" for it. Of course, we never know what actually will happen, and that is exciting. In the beginning, this takes getting used to.

There are even more changes. Instead of gnawing self-centeredness, we feel attached to many of the people we have met in the program; they have become terribly important to us. Because they have come to know us and to let us know them, they have given us the opportunity to live in new ways. They have become the mirror in which we are able to see ourselves without turning away. Through them, we have come to love things in ourselves we never could have loved without them. Beginning to care about ourselves has helped us make the passage through some very difficult seas of self-discovery.

To our amazement, those new gay and straight friends in the program have been there for us when we least expected it. They have become loving companions, even when we have traveled to other cities on business or on a holiday. They never abandoned or deserted us. "Keep coming back" they always told us—no matter what we told them. They have traveled with us through some harrowing places, and because of their concern and love, we have learned it is possible to live a different way. Instead of finding ourselves alone in early recovery, we have been surrounded by a great company of survivors who can live sober lives—with the support of one another. We have the evidence now that sobriety is possible for us because we have already *lived through* sober experiences together.

The Need for Personal Inventory

Why, then, do we need to begin working on Step Ten? Isn't all that "old stuff" behind us? Haven't we proved we can live without alcohol or drugs, as well as other addictive habits? What is the point of stirring things up in lives that have finally settled down? Having already gone through an inventory of secrets and people, why do we need to begin working on a *daily* inventory of ourselves? Many of the people who find this suggestion most irritating also discover themselves taking recovery more and more for granted in their lives.

This Step is not an exercise designed for victims who need grist for their suffering mill. The effects of alcoholism, and of every addiction, remain with us in recovery: "Alcoholism is an '*ism*' not a '*wasm*.'" But unless we understand how this applies to and operates in our lives, with our own material, we begin to take it for granted. In time, we forget it. Forgetting and denial are first cousins.

The inventories we wrote in Steps Four and Eight have revealed many things that otherwise would have continued to feed our patterns of denial. By bringing these crucial aspects of ourselves into the light, by confronting the past and the way we lived it, we have learned to live through all we have done instead of needing to escape from it. In Step Ten, we begin using the same technique on the present, on our daily lives just as we live them. We begin to see what we do, and how we interpret it, in today.

Each of the three inventory Steps has to do directly with raising our level of consciousness about people, places and things, and our relationship with them. Both as children and as alcoholics, we were oblivious to anything more than being carried away with what-happened-next and taking for granted that something "next" would happen. Some of us may still retain vivid memories of a great deal that went on then. In our addiction, however, many of us have had blackouts in which we remember nothing about anything, or "brownouts" in which we have only blurred recollections we cannot be certain of. Recovery calls for developing a new manner of living, and taking a daily inventory of our lives is one way of accepting responsibility for continuing to grow in sobriety instead of taking it for granted. This inventory provides us with a useful tool for showing up for our lives today with the person we are becoming.

Revealing ourselves *to* ourselves raises our level of consciousness. With the enhancement that this perspective of our lives gives us, we get many new insights about both recovery and the old habits we developed in addiction. Among the first things we notice is that many of the same problems that beset us in the past are still with us in the present! Problems having to do with anger, envy, control, self-pity, intimacy continue to come up for us, and they still throw us off balance. They can ruin our day, and prevent us from sleeping at night, as well.

In recovery, we need to face these problems and learn to deal with them, because our journey continues *through* these confrontations, not around them. Does this voice sound familiar? "Is this what I got clean and sober for?" "Why is it that when things get screwed up in my life, I'm always around?" "Back again to square one! Damn it!" "What a disappointment! Do I need a better reason to pick up and use again?" This is addictive thinking that pounds at us through that critical voice and tries to push us back into destructive behavior. For all of us, changing the critical voice to a loving one can be one of the biggest hurdles of sobriety.

We did not drink or use over nothing. Whatever the reasons were, our addiction made every one of them worse. Through our efforts to work the Twelve-Step program, we have discovered that we are able to live without whatever substance we abused. Now, we need to prove to ourselves that we can survive the problems as well, no matter what they are. In recovery, few of our old problems—employment, relationships, housing—have disappeared; they have been waiting for us to resolve. Many of us are thrown into confusion when we start to work at solutions to these problems. Addiction has played havoc in our lives, and facing this can be very disorienting. It is helpful to remind ourselves of this continually instead of dismissing it.

We have survived a catastrophe and are now recuperating from it. Our attitude toward ourselves in the midst of this transition is important. We need to be loving and understanding. We need to learn new ways to help ourselves through dark moments and to appreciate our efforts and accomplishments even as we struggle with our obstacles. This takes being committed to ourselves and to our willingness to change. By loving ourselves and giving up being critical of ourselves, we begin to do this.

This new attitude of support is entirely different from the self-pity we are familiar with. Supporting ourselves makes us a friend to ourselves instead of an enemy. In our addiction, we were our own enemy when we used our energy and the energy of others to fragment and destroy ourselves. Now, our challenge is to use this energy to grow and to create a new life. And instead of making obstacles of ourselves, we have learned about the process of acceptance and what it means to live through that process.

Loving Ourselves

Many gay men and lesbians have years of experience withholding love from themselves (and rejecting others as well). Becoming a friend to ourselves takes time. We have become sober, but that doesn't mean that either we or the world have become loving. Because we are the source, we are the ones who must introduce this love through our own efforts—both with ourselves and with other people.

Like a bellows from which an addictive perspective has been gradually emptied and then refilled with sober, healthy ideas, our lives have breathed extremes. We have been learning and relearning how to be loving and patient, how to be our own friend. There is no protocol for doing this; in each situation it has to be created out of all the elements present.

One requirement, however, is basic: it is never possible to create a new life when we are our own enemy. Only through the integration of all our conflicting wishes and abilities is it possible to live creatively in new ways. Step Ten provides us with a great deal of the information that we need about our wishes and abilities. These data form the basis on which to build a new inner relationship that is the foundation for positive self-caring.

We will be amazed, when we work on this Step, to discover how we have begun using our energy in so many different directions. Feeling healthier and better grounded emotionally than we ever did during our addiction, we have taken on many new responsibilities that make conflicting demands on our time and resources. We have become involved with new friends in the program and some, perhaps, not in the program. Many of us are back working at old jobs, or new ones, and we have found ourselves once again in contact with family. Emerging from the isolation of addiction, we have encountered people, places and things that push our buttons in many of the same old ways as before. As a result, we feel at cross-purposes some of the time—knowing what we should do, yet acting differently. It is good to know that the help we need to handle this is the help we get from working Step Ten.

There is a way to prevent ourselves from being completely carried away by the cross-purposes that vie for our energy. Through a daily willingness to examine what is going on in our lives, it is possible to gain a clearer perspective on ourselves. In recovery, many things happen to us and to others we care about, and we react. Instead of fastening ourselves to these events, to these reactions out of which we make obstacles, as if it were only by doing this that we had any reality, we can choose to separate from them. Listing them in our inventory, we may discover that we have stopped at these obstacles only because it appears that we have reached our limit. The truth is that we have reached *their* limit, and, with the efforts we have been learning to make in our program, we can use our energy to pass through them.

We have asked others to treat us differently in recovery, and we must learn to do the same ourselves. Do we even have any idea how to do this? The daily inventory creates a dialogue with ourselves that encourages communication about what is going right and what is going wrong. Everything laid out in it reveals to us what works and what doesn't. In the past, we lived from disaster to disaster. Now, instead of waiting until a disaster strikes, we can begin to learn to recognize danger signals early and to take the appropriate steps before situations get out of hand.

Becoming our own friend is an active process in which we also stay honest with ourselves. We don't keep secrets any longer—not even from ourselves—and Step Ten provides us with a pattern of new behavior.

Without realizing it, we began developing this opportunity in Step Four. Whether we did it a long time ago or recently, most of us left out a great deal on the first inventory. I have never met anyone who has taken a "perfect" Step Four. Nevertheless, what we wrote at that time in our journey was all we were capable to recording. It was crucial for our recovery that we did it, for it cleared out space in which we could develop new and sober patterns. If we will use Step Ten as it is intended, we can continue to have the benefit of more and more working space in which to grow.

Monitoring Perfectionism

As we look at ourselves each day from the perspective of what we need to do in order to grow, we support ourselves in dealing with one of our major shortcomings: perfectionism. Alcoholics in recovery struggle with this problem no matter how long we are clean and sober. Even though we are constantly reminded not to "take other people's inventories," we do it anyway. Perhaps it has caused resentment here and there, or even serious rifts in new relationships. This perfectionism is a pattern we have grown up with, and it stays with us in recovery until we practice getting rid of it. When we take responsibility for ourselves, we don't have the energy or the impetus for blaming others.

As critical as we can be of other people, it merely takes some of the heat off ourselves. We are constantly comparing ourselves with others even though we have been told how counterproductive it is. Do any of us ever think we have progressed as far as we *should* have in our program? Even though our index finger may point at other people, three other fingers on our hand are always pointing back at ourselves. Most of us are even oblivious to how frequently we do it, and that is one of the old habits Step Ten can reveal.

In recovery, we need to develop new behaviors to replace the old ones. As each of the other Steps before this has suggested, we have to learn to use our own experience in order to progress. As each of us has learned through sharing at meetings, our experience *can* benefit others. In Step Ten, we can begin, in a very conscious manner, to allow this same experience to benefit *ourselves*. We can monitor our perfectionism by taking a daily inventory of it.

None of us is perfect, nor should we be. Yet we think of ourselves and criticize ourselves as if we should be. It is no wonder that we continue to function at cross-purposes. Completing a daily inventory grounds us with the evidence we need in order to continue our journey in recovery instead of turning off and getting lost again in "stinking thinking." No matter how long we have abstained from the "cunning, baffling and powerful" substances we used, they still wait for us to pick them up again. They affect our minds, and our thoughts play tricks on us. It is all too easy for us to find ourselves going off on mental tangents that, if pursued far enough, would end in substance abuse.

Instead of getting lost in these thoughts, we can look at the evidence that a daily inventory provides us:

- What have we done, and how are we reacting to it?
- What did we plan to do, and what have we put off doing?
- What problems and what solutions have we found in relating honestly with other people?
- What new secrets, obstacles, and limitations have shown up in our lives?
- What can we be grateful for?

The answers provide us with the evidence we need in order to put this quest for perfectionism into proper perspective.

Step Ten concludes, ". . . and when we were wrong, promptly admitted it." The perfectionist in each one of us needs this direction. It reminds us that more important than being right is admitting when we are wrong. The victim attitude leaves us always with a terror of making mistakes, and with the fear of failure as well as the fear of success. Addicts have carried this unbearable burden around with them their entire lives. It is the root cause of inaction, escape, depression and despair. In addiction, the use of substances provided relief from these fears because it deadened or anesthetized feelings for a time. But that relief ultimately ended. Like everything else we tried, using alcohol or drugs turned into just another mistake.

No one likes either to make or to admit mistakes. In recovery, we need to change the rule that mistakes mean we have failed and that we are worthless human beings. In place of this, we can give ourselves permission to make as many mistakes as we need to every day of our lives. It is only by changing our rules in this way that we can experience ourselves as imperfect beings. We can stop trying to live some dream of perfection that truly does not work in reality. We know that it does not work, because we have tried it in our addiction. No matter how high we managed to get, the elevator of depression was always there to take us further and further down.

If we are going to be alive in recovery, we are going to make mistakes. Step Ten provides us with a "safety net" to prevent us from becoming overwhelmed by these mistakes. From our old habit of keeping secrets, we know that we *will* be overwhelmed unless we reveal them. Promptly admitting our mistakes, both to ourselves and to others, prevents us from being overwhelmed by them. Neither the world nor any one of us falls apart when we do it. That is recovery!

Action Instead of Reaction

The essential elements of the Twelve-Step programs were encapsulated once for me in these three simple sentences: "Things happen. I react to them. Life goes on." In recovery, we can learn to act on our behalf instead of merely reacting to others. There is a big change in us when we do this. We learn how to live in a new way through the efforts we make to act, rather than react, each day.

Often, we are confused by what goes on around us, and rarely can we see order in any of it. But we have lived long enough in our illusions to know that fantasy does not provide us with what we seek. It is the evidence that appears in our daily inventories that points the way. Understanding and accepting the experience of our lives, as far as we are willing to be conscious of it, is the help we need in order to get on with the task. Confronting the things that happen to us—when they happen—and taking action to deal with the problems created, makes it possible for us to go on with our lives in a healthy manner.

Many people are willing to work on all of the Steps except this one. Step Ten requires the kind of self-discipline and vigilance that we wish in others but excuse in ourselves. We need to realize that by doing Step Ten each day, we will find that many of our problems will no longer be problems. Some people actually make a list. Others discuss their day with a sponsor, friend, lover, or therapist or at a meeting. Still others set apart some quiet time to take an unhurried look at the events of the day. It seems that many of us would rather suffer with our problems than make a daily inventory that could give us insight into solving them. The pattern of suffering is hardest of all to break, but it is not as difficult as we imagine.

One night last year, I was riding on a shuttle bus in Yosemite National Park. Suddenly, I heard the driver announce: "This bus is leaving Stop Eight, Yosemite Lodge, and will not be returning. This is the last bus tonight. Please deal with this fact *now*; do not wait until later!" I thought of Step Ten, which invites all of us to deal with what is going right and what is going wrong in our lives each day. Continuing on our journey depends on making this choice.

We find ourselves back again at the question of priorities. Step Ten not only provides us with assistance in setting priorities for dealing with our problems, it also becomes a priority in our recovery—when we make it one. The paradox is waiting for us: out of the disorder that shows up in our daily inventory, it is possible to begin to live in harmony with ourselves. We "keep it simple" when we establish priorities for dealing with our problems.

GUIDES TO PROGRESS

"You shouldn't have told her to mind her own business." "You really made a pig of yourself at dinner last night." "You never go out for coffee with good-looking women; you always stick with the trolls." "You've got to do something about your hair; it's disgusting." "You'll end up in this lousy job for the rest of your life unless you go back to school." "Why can't you stick up for yourself when you get put on the carpet by that jerk you've got for a boss?" "How long has it been since you went out on a date with a woman with as much sobriety as you've got?" "Did you think your mother was going to send you a bouquet just because you got your three-year anniversary chip?" The committee went on and on in Celie's mind, and she was getting sick of the sound of their voices. "Will you all please SHUT UP?" she said suddenly. And they did. They could always start up again, but she had come to understand that she was really in charge; she could silence them any time she wanted to if she just did it.

Ted had a very busy legal practice. He always wore conservative clothes and was very careful never to let the slightest trace of his gayness reveal itself in his speech and mannerisms. After seven months in AA, during which he always went to meetings in the city instead of in the suburb where he lived, he heard about a gay meeting and decided to go. He left his jacket and tie in the car and wore a sweater over his button-down shirt. It was only after one of the most flamboyantly dressed men had spoken that Ted realized he wished he could be as comfortable about his life as that man was. That level of acceptance was something he wanted for himself. Though he didn't have to speak in that tone of voice, or wear pink pants or a feather earring, he could still listen to what the man said and apply it to his life. The breakthrough for him was that he understood his approval meant absolutely nothing, but that his acceptance—of the others in the room *and* himself—meant everything. He drove back to the suburbs after getting a few telephone numbers, including one from the man with the feather earring.

Suggestions for Action

At home, we look into the mirror several times a day. Sometimes, on the street, we catch a glimpse of ourselves in a store window. Set aside five minutes each day, alone, in which you can be with yourself in front of a mirror, and, instead of being critical, learn to be loyal to what you see there. Affirm yourself with words that support your efforts in recovery.

REFLECTIONS

When we ride too many of our wishes, we can be thrown by them. When we set our sights on one wish—recovery—we move steadily in that direction.

Step Eleven

ANTIDOTE TO EGOCENTRICITY

CONDITION: SELF-CENTEREDNESS

In addiction, alcoholics are fruitlessly in search of self-satisfaction. They are self-seekers above all. There is no possibility of creating a bond with another human being as long as alcohol inflates the ego with denial and the illusion of self-sufficiency.

ALTERNATIVE: SPIRITUAL BONDING

Recovery opens the way to relate with others through sharing instead of using, through appreciation instead of only gratification, and through intimacy, because self-revelation (instead of dishonesty and secrecy) is required.

Experiencing the presence of a power greater than ourselves, we understand that we did not create this presence on our own. We begin to consciously strive for a connection with this Higher Power to ensure the continuation of the benefits we have already received.

STEP ELEVEN:

Sought through prayer and meditation to improve our conscious contact with God *as we understood God,* praying only for knowledge of God's will for us and the power to carry that out.

Our path through early recovery has never been easy, in spite of the remarkably simple directions that the Steps make available to us. When we have been willing to follow these suggestions, we have confronted and passed through major obstacles of our lives. The perfectionist in each of us, along with the victim, the isolator, the manipulator, and the people-pleaser, has undergone some change. Being honest with ourselves has raised our level of consciousness about who we are, what we do, and what happens when we take responsibility for our actions.

Creating Balance

Changing our own relationship with ourselves and with other people is an ongoing process that shapes new developments every day of our lives. We may often feel as if the emotional swings we experience have landed us in extremely uncomfortable situations; nevertheless, we discover that we no longer remain stuck in them. There is movement, and there is space in which to make our way forward, or in any other direction. The longer we experience recovery, the more room we have in which to make choices that affirm us as responsible gay men and lesbians.

As the years have passed, it is always a surprise for me when I meet the man who drank. Most of the time, this has happened not when I'm feeling depressed or troubled but when I am feeling terrific, when I am very high on life. This alcoholic-I in me usually appears when no dark clouds sit on my horizon and my focus is above the treetops delighting in the blue sky. When he shows up, I discover that he has slipped into my relaxed mind because he feels safe enough to come out of hiding. Many others in recovery have had the same experience, and we have shared the shock of it together. What seems clear is that the space for growth that we have created in our lives will always be filled with something. Our old patterns are ready to intrude when a vacuum develops.

Recovery is a different way to live. When we consider the way we lived in our addiction, we now have a great deal to compare it with. In place of the fragmentation and isolation of our old lives, we understand that we can create balance through working on the Steps each day. Let's remember that extremes will always be waiting out there for us, and that our opportunity in sobriety is to choose to create balance instead of hurling headlong in any direction.

In the beginning, we have little or no idea what balance means. Through the efforts we make working each of the Steps, we introduce our bodies, emotions and intellects to this concept. For each of us, along with the efforts we need to make in order to experience it day by day, balance has a very personal meaning.

From deprivation and *im*balance, from being out of control and being swept away by our addiction, we discover that the energy we create each day can be directed into action that affirms and supports our recovery. What seemed to be the impossible has gradually become reality. We have turned our lives around. Taking an honest look at ourselves, we find we have convincing evidence that tells us we will continue to make progress as long as we are willing to work the Steps.

Acting As-If

All of us began without this evidence that progress was possible, and, at that time, we were encouraged to act as if we had it. Journeying through the first ten Steps, we have accumulated a great deal of evidence of progress. Now, it is essential for us to begin to work through something many of us either avoided or simply refused to confront earlier—our relationship with a Higher Power, with a power greater than ourselves, no matter what we choose to call that source of energy.

Acting as-if required us to make a conscious decision. Even though we may have strongly resisted the idea of a power greater than ourselves, by acting as if it existed, we found ourselves relieved of the crushing burden of isolation. Without this burden, we were able to emerge from behind the barriers of bigotry and shame with which religion isolates and humiliates gay men and lesbians. No longer alone, we found ourselves standing amid the multitude of men and women in recovery everywhere. We participated with all of them in the healing power of the group in action. The spiritual dimension of our lives unfurled. To our amazement, we experienced the presence of a Higher Power in some of the most inaccessible areas of our being. Many of us neither understood how this happened nor chose to call the source of it by name.

For agnostics, atheists, or fallen-away Catholics, Protestants, and Jews, this was something of a miracle! We found ourselves the beneficiaries of a healing power in our lives even though we may have been reluctant to do anything more than act as if this energy were there. We saw, gradually, that our connection with this force had very little, if anything, to do with our old ideas about religion or God, ideas that had been furnished and maintained by the homophobic society in which we grew up. That each one of us could experience his or her own connection with the spiritual dimension, apart from any church or doctrine, was a revelation that was waiting for us in our recovery.

The conscious decision to act as-if brought results. We drank from a cup that always seemed to have been forbidden to us, and unlike any of the other substances we had used before, during, and after our addiction, we did not find escape from life but *connection* with it. Something began to happen within us each time we heard the beginning of Chapter 5 from the Big Book, "How It Works," and with each Serenity Prayer or other prayer we said. We laid a certain groundwork in our lives that had not been there before—no matter how devout we might have been in the past. We were preparing something within us that invited spiritual concerns and awareness to reprogram our old patterns of thought and action.

We began with little things, and then, with larger ones, we found ourselves more accessible to spiritual ideas. The egocentricity of our lives as alcoholics began to undergo modification. Instead of the fruitless pursuit of self-satisfaction, we discovered something happening to us in the meeting rooms and in our own daily lives that was taking its place. When we showed up for life in recovery, we found ourselves involved daily in caring for and loving ourselves and other people just because we were open to it and not because we were going to get something in return. In this process, we discovered that we had somehow gotten out of our own way and were connecting with life instead of being its victim. This connection, with ourselves and with others, is spiritual.

It is much more difficult to attempt to disguise ourselves as victims after a spiritual connection with a Higher Power has been made in our lives. We cannot get away with the old habits of self-pity and self-sabotage when we have forged links that, by their nature, indicate we are worthwhile human beings. Garbage doesn't have a Higher Power. Acting as if we are worthy to receive help, we received it, and there is no one among us who could deny the evidence of recovery if we are honest.

Raising Our Consciousness

The last three Steps are each concerned with raising our level of consciousness about the essential elements of our lives as gay men and lesbians in the world of recovery. Step Ten focused on ourselves, our personhood: who we are, how we are, and what it is like to live inside our body, emotions and intellect. Developing this higher level of consciousness of ourselves through a daily inventory, we have used our own experience to learn to live honestly and productively instead of rocketing back and forth "off the wall" of our possibilities.

In Step Eleven, we direct our attention to raising our level of consciousness about a Higher Power—"*as we understand*" this power greater than ourselves. The italics appear in the text of the Step itself to remind us that we are to do this with the *new* understanding we have been developing in recovery, not the old ideas we operated with in our addiction.

Just as we benefited earlier from making the conscious decision to act as if this power existed, so will we progress much further in our journey by seeking "through prayer and meditation to improve our conscious contact" with this power. No matter how long we resist, through the experience of our recovery we come to acknowledge and accept some kind of experience that can be called either a spiritual awakening or a spiritual connection within ourselves.

It is remarkable how many people, both gay and straight, make the same comment after they have spent time in a Twelve-Step program: "When I first walked through the door, if anyone had told me that I was going to have to start to pray or meditate, I would have turned around and walked out!" Many of us, I think, can remember back to that time and admit we too were unable to hear very much else then—except the distinct message that we didn't have to go on killing ourselves with our addiction. In what others said to us, we heard hope, even if we weren't able to catch all the rest of the words, and we kept coming back. That is how we began the journey, and from that beginning we now find ourselves at Step Eleven.

Over and over we have heard the Twelve Steps read at the beginning of a meeting. The words of each Step were carefully repeated, but how many of us ever thought they were meant for *me*? With the room filled with so many people, it was easy to make this mistake. Listening to the repetition of the Steps and hearing the words as our minds became clearer, we have begun to realize that each Step follows the previous one in a progressive sequence that reflects stages of recovery. It is precisely for this reason that it is suggested we work them in order—at least that we *start* them in order, it not actually complete them. More important than the order is the fact that we work them.

Until we have spent time, effort and energy on a Step, we are not prepared to go on to the next one. It is usually suggested that when we reach a Step we are having particular difficulty with, we should go back to the one before it to work on, in conjunction with the basics: Steps One, Two and Three. A great deal of "unfinished business" can be cleared away by returning to an earlier Step. After we deal with some of these loose ends, we discover ourselves available to continue with the Step we balked at doing.

Because it is an individual program, we must work on the Steps at our own speed. Recovery is not a race; it is a journey. We cannot get ahead of ourselves without running the risk of "slipping"—picking up and using old solutions that were part of our addiction. We are reminded, as well, never to compare our progress with anyone else's, or even an earlier period of our own sobriety with our present experience. By staying with who we are now, it is possible to leave the past behind instead of living in it. This is the support we can give ourselves rather than falling back into the old patterns of self-criticism and perfectionism.

For those who are ready for it, for those who find themselves in recovery asking, "Is there something more?" Step Eleven provides what we need in order to proceed on our journey.

The better we have come to know ourselves, to honestly reveal who we are to others and to ourselves, the better we have prepared ourselves to live in a different relationship with life in our recovery.

Without this knowledge and understanding of ourselves, we lack the connections essential for the development of new and healthy patterns of thought and action. Without them, we are unprepared for a change in our availability to relate with a power greater than ourselves. The health that we, as well as others, observe returning to our bodies and our emotions has been obvious. What is far less obvious is that the development of our physical and emotional well-being creates a new capacity for spiritual growth along with it. The evidence of this is that we find ourselves no longer "shut down" but, instead, experiencing the wonder of living almost as though we were children once again.

We should never underestimate the spiritual deprivation of our lives as gay and lesbian alcoholics. Our intense physical and emotional isolation, terror, guilt, and shame during addiction was deepened by our spiritual bankruptcy. Our self-seeking in relationships and jobs was rooted in survival, and our overwhelming fear of failure or rule of perfectionism damned us in every area of our lives. Even though we had low self-esteem, we were still the center of the universe. And, at the end, there was absolutely no one to turn to—not even God! We were abandoned by everyone, including ourselves.

The first effort we had to make to change this was the acknowledgment of our predicament; we had to take the first Step. It was only after doing this that it was possible for help to reach us. Until we were entirely convinced that our lives were unmanageable, we stubbornly persisted in trying to manage them. Many of us experienced what it was like to be truly vulnerable, in that early stage of sobriety, and instead of feeling abandoned, we found ourselves nurtured and supported. Other people just like ourselves were there for us. What seemed at least as incredible as this at the time was that they needed *us* as much as we needed them. All of us found that we had something valuable to offer even as we received support from others.

From the knowledge and understanding we have about the incredible journey all of us make into recovery, it seems clear that our experience of a Higher Power begins from the moment we reach out to help another suffering addict with our own vulnerability. The more efforts we make to reach out, the stronger and deeper is the bond we develop between ourselves and higher forces in the world. As bearers of these forces, we become a vital channel for them to function in our own lives as well as in the lives of others. Moreover, in serving as a channel, we receive the healing benefit ourselves. Through our efforts, we give ourselves a gift that none of our self-seeking could have achieved. It is a paradox that recovery is revealed to us not in some unusual psychic experience but as we live it every day.

Life After Addiction

We did not set out on our journey to serve others; we came through the door because we did not want to die. We did as others in the recovery programs told us, not because we understood the reason but because we did not want to die. With little faith or hope left in us, we began to work the Steps, not because we believed in them but because we did not want to die. It seems appropriate, now that we discover that we are not going to die—that there *is* life after addiction—to ask ourselves, What are we going to do with our lives?

It took me quite some time in recovery to ask myself this question. Not long afterward, someone I was speaking with helped me to understand something that had never occurred to me:

God has a unique purpose for your life. Find it! Do it!

The man who said this to me had been in a Twelve-Step program for over thirty years. In the period I had known him, this was the first time I had ever heard him mention God, and I was so startled that I could hardly believe my ears. For all my years of living with the implicit belief in my own uniqueness, this was the first time I connected this idea about myself with a Higher Power. The possibility of a Higher Power needing *me*—after recovery efforts had helped me to understand I was not unique—was a breakthrough into a totally different understanding of Step Eleven than had ever occurred to me. For some reason I could not explain, the connection was difficult to hold on to. By writing it down, however, I found that I could allow it to be, without my getting in the way.

I am not unique; I am unique!

At the heart of this paradox is an insight about aloneness identical to what comes after working on Step Two in early recovery. At that time, it was not possible to be concerned with anything more than the devastating effects of addiction. In recovery, however, after working on the first ten Steps, we have prepared the foundation to see ourselves as *capable* of living fully and completely instead of waiting, like victims, for death to find us and take us out of our misery. With both a present *and* a future, like everyone else who lives in recovery, all of us have choices to make that will inevitably reflect our own individual nature—our uniqueness and our *un*-uniqueness.

Thinking back to what our lives were like at the beginning of our journey, back in Step Two, we will remember how we found ourselves caught between the two extremes: "I am alone; I am not alone." Instead of remaining stuck, we were encouraged to attend Twelve-Step meetings and become part of a group of people just like ourselves—recovering alcoholics. Our initial efforts to interact with the group created the way out of our addiction and began our journey into health. This happened only because we were willing to take this action. To break out of our isolation, we needed to use our energy to connect with others around us. This required conscious effort; we had to choose to do this for ourselves, no matter how many reasons to resist presented themselves.

We have come much further in our journey into recovery, and we have learned a great deal more about ourselves and other people along the way. We have become far more conscious of our own actions and theirs than ever before in our lives. It is with this better developed understanding of ourselves that Step Eleven now directs us to "improve our conscious contact" with a Higher Power. The reason is basic. Just as using our energy to connect with the group introduced balance into lives that had been polarized and fragmented by addiction, so using our energy to connect with a Higher Power introduces the balance we need now and in the future to pursue our progress in recovery.

Through a conscious effort to improve our connection with a power greater than ourselves, we discover the way to set in balance those extremes that, no matter how far along we are in recovery, are always waiting for us. Our willingness to become available to a spiritual connection in our lives makes us a channel for resolving the conflict and confusion that can arise at any time. Through prayer and meditation, we are able to create a pattern we can use no matter what the crisis or the victory. Relying on this pattern, we will be able to introduce balance in our lives.

Back then, in the pain, in the despair and disappointment of addiction, we turned to the group for help. Some of us identified the group with a Higher Power; others did not. Now, from this vastly different place in ourselves, we know beyond a shadow of a doubt that we have not made this journey alone or without help.

Prayer and Meditation

Prayer is one of the ways we have of consciously recognizing this understanding within ourselves. Just as honesty provides us with a foundation for living in harmony with others, so prayer can create in us a spiritual foundation for living in harmony with ourselves.

For many of us, petitions for things and apologies for ourselves have figured heavily in the words we said when we have tried to use the old patterns of praying that were given to us when we were children. In recovery, we need to be honest in our prayers about who we are now, instead of who we were, and about what we bring to the dialogue—our strengths along with our weaknesses. As gay men and lesbians, we need to use words that reveal who we are in recovery. For each of us, this can mean many things. Walt Whitman reminds us of something essential to this revelation of ourselves in these few lines from "*Salut Au Monde.*"

> Each of us inevitable,
> Each of us limitless—each of us with his or her right upon the earth,
> Each of us allow'd the eternal purports of the earth,
> Each of us here as divinely as any is here.

Unless we credit ourselves with these entitlements, we withhold ourselves from the healing experience of prayer that is waiting for us in recovery.

Through prayer and meditation we can find our voice. No matter how long it takes us to develop the courage to speak with it, we need to learn to do this. Only when we speak with our own voice can we stop pretending we are more or less than ourselves. And, by accepting ourselves, along with everything that is and everything that is not, we make ourselves available to receiving support for living and changing. Only our own words, based on our own personal experience of honesty and gratitude for our lives, will open the way to a spiritual dialogue, which begins the moment we are silent. After we have spoken and are ready to listen, the connection with a Higher Power can begin.

The story of our addiction was "self-will run riot." The account of our recovery is waiting for us to write. A day at a time, we are learning to live with uncertainty about what this new life is all about. Egocentric behavior is part of old patterns that the Steps help us to recognize. In sobriety, we have the choice to act differently. With the new patterns of thinking and acting that we are developing, with the support of friends and sponsors and family who accept us in recovery, we create each new day out of the willingness to continue the journey.

Through prayer and meditation, the development of a spiritual bond with ourselves, with other people and with God/Higher Power enriches our lives each day with greater self-esteem than any of our empty triumphs ever gained us. The evidence of this will appear as we create a sober history for ourselves over the months and years ahead. We did not secure the benefits of sobriety in one day or one week. The evidence of the benefits of spiritual bonding will only be revealed in time.

The effect of spiritual bonding on our life is powerful. Prayer and meditation work. Gay men and lesbians who develop a spiritual connection experience a far deeper serenity than those who choose to omit Step Eleven from their recovery. Not only would we, as individuals, be different without it, but so would each of the Twelve-Step programs be incomplete as well. Through the conscious efforts we make to be a channel for higher forces, of a God or a Higher Power, the narrow path of our journey through early recovery broadens into an open freeway on which each of us will experience the promises of the program.

In the Big Book of Alcoholics Anonymous, these promises are articulated with great care and directness. They show us our way into the future:

If we are painstaking about this phase of our development, we will be amazed before we are half way through. We are going to know a new freedom and a new happiness. We will not regret the past nor wish to shut the door on it.

We will comprehend the word serenity and we will know peace. No matter how far down the scale we have gone, we will see how our experience can benefit others. That feeling of uselessness and self-pity will disappear. We will lose interest in selfish things and gain interest in our fellows.

Self-seeking will slip away. Our whole attitude and outlook upon life will change. Fear of people and of economic insecurity will leave us. We will intuitively know how to handle situations which used to baffle us. We will suddenly realize that God is doing for us what we could not do for ourselves.

Are these extravagant promises? We think not. They are being fulfilled among us—sometimes quickly, sometimes slowly. They will always material-ize if we work for them.*

Step Eleven supports us each step of the way—if we work it!

---

*Alcoholics Anonymous, 83-84.

GUIDES TO PROGRESS

There are a variety of approaches on this issue. There just is no one way to find God. There's a guy I knew who used to say that the major gift of the program to him was that it helped him to find his own peace with his own God in his own way. I like that expression. The fact is that each of us has to do this separately, no matter how much we may share in common about the attitude and the will of God. We've got to come up with our own concept of what God is so that it works for us. I've often had trouble with what I call the "magic" approach to God; by that I mean there are people who say when X happens, then "that's the will of God." This makes it sound as if God's will is everything that does indeed happen in the world. I've always had trouble with that point of view. Thank you very much, but I don't want the God who allowed Auschwitz to happen; I don't want the God who allows Thalidomide babies; I don't want the God who allows AIDS. I don't understand the will of God, but what I do understand is that I have to be on a path that requires a deepening understanding of what God's will is in *my* life—not necessarily the whole place of human nature. I don't believe at all in the "magic" approach—that God helps certain people find parking places, and others he doesn't; God helps some people win the lottery, and others he doesn't. For me, that sort of thing is offensive. What's really important is to emphasize the varieties of experience that are possible in order for us to come to terms with the kind of God we want in our lives. [David A.]

This morning, I opened one of the meditation books I have, and it said, "He led me." I know this is a spiritual program, and I hear that all the time. But every time I see or hear words like that, I get very angry. I was in the convent for eleven years, and I dealt with that kind of spirituality. I find it sometimes in AA, and I find it in Al-Anon. I am not that kind of spiritual person. But I am spiritual. I do not have a "He" in my life. All right. I do not have an in-quotes "G-O-D." I do not say the Our Father, but I *do* take your hand . . . and I get together with you, and when I take your hand and we connect with each other, then I'm stronger. But I will not give this away. I will not say that I am no good, and that I must be filled with another being in order to be good. Because I *am* good, and *you* are good. You are my God and I am yours. I revolt from the He. There are many times that I cringe inside because some of you seem to be saying that if only I come around long enough, and am honest enough, that I will find what you have. And I say to you that I already have it. I am giving mine to you. I cannot be a recovering person on my own. . . . I need all the gay men and lesbians in these programs, because together we recover our spirit. [Helen K.]

Suggestions for Action

After you have become well grounded in one of the Twelve-Step programs, it is possible that you will discover the appropriateness of other Twelve-Step programs in your recovery. Attend a few of these meetings with the intention of expanding your sobriety to include it—but not at the risk of losing it.

REFLECTIONS

To be ready for change, we need to prepare ourselves physically, emotionally and mentally. Growth depends on our readiness to grow.

Step Twelve

COMMUNITY AND SERVICE

CONDITION: SELF-SEEKING

In the gay bars where some of us spent our time, there was laughter but not an abundance of joy. We looked everywhere for something to fill the void inside ourselves. Our search focused more and more on selfish things; even these disappointed us. The more we got, the less satisfied we were. We became desperate.

ALTERNATIVE: COMMUNION AND SERVICE

With acceptance of ourselves, with faith that we can find happiness, with surrender to a power greater than ourselves, with honesty and vulnerability and self-revelation, and with flexibility and humility we enter into community. We can find joy in recovery even in the dingiest of church basements.

This community is an environment for healing. We have been invited into this experience of healing because we are exactly who we are—recovering gay men and lesbians. We understand that in sharing with others, our own process is accelerated.

STEP TWELVE:

Having had a spiritual awakening as the result of these steps, we tried to carry this message to alcoholics, and to practice these principles in all our affairs.

The moment we walked through the door of any Twelve-Step program, we began practicing Step Twelve. Even though we may not have understood its full significance, all of us have been carrying the message of recovery and participating in the process it initiates.

"Twelve-Stepping"

Each time we share our lives with others, we "twelve-step" them as well as ourselves. As much as anyone else, we need to hear ourselves talk about what has happened to us and how we feel about it. From sharing the details of our addiction and recovery comes the support *we* need. We continue receiving the benefits of Twelve-Step programs as we take advantage of the opportunity to reveal and acknowledge to others our vulnerability and imperfection, along with our progress.

There is a large contingent of people in recovery who admit they are alcoholics and then jump immediately into the task of reaching out to others, without working any of the Steps between One and Twelve. They base their entire program exclusively on telling their story, and they cheat themselves and those they want to help because they skipped all of their own growing from Steps Two through Eleven. We cannot give it away unless we first have it. It is vitally important to our recovery that we stick with the real "winners"—people who have actually "walked the walk" instead of only "talking the talk."

Many of us seriously believed, at the beginning of our journey, that we could go to a few meetings and get "fixed" by a program. By the time we get to Step Twelve, however, we understand that the idea of getting "fixed" was part of our addiction and has nothing to do with recovery. No one ever gets "fixed" by anyone else. Instead, we share our stories of what it was like, what happened, and what it's like now. Then, we "turn it over." In the process of doing this, we find new support and hope inside ourselves, as well as from others, because we were willing to risk. Through the effort to share comes the realization that no one has to die from the problems of alcoholism. That is the message we bring to others and to ourselves; that is the work that is always waiting for us to do.

Because we easily forget this responsibility to ourselves, other people constantly remind us of the two essential actions we must take to remain sober and clean: "Don't drink or use! *And go to meetings!*" Our journey begins with this, but we must work through every one of the Steps to find out what the rest of recovery really means.

There are no short cuts to Step Twelve. We are ready for it only *after* we have been through the process laid out in the first eleven Steps. Only through the efforts we make can we begin to understand who we are and how we can grow. No matter how many insights we may have about ourselves, we do not suddenly emerge into deeper self-understanding the moment we put down the drink or the drug. The damage we have suffered physically, emotionally, intellectually and spiritually requires time to be healed. We deceive ourselves if we believe otherwise.

As alcoholics, we lived in the isolation of our dreams and the extremes of our fantasies. Addiction excluded us from everything except the company of other addicts; we were incapable of relationships. Had we not walked through the door of one of the Twelve-Step programs, we would probably have remained like that.

Alone, we would have succumbed to addiction. By finding a recovery program where there were others just like ourselves suffering from the effects of the disease, we began our journey through the wilderness. The intensity of the isolation we experienced was relieved by attending meetings where others shared feelings identical to ours. Many of us thought it miraculous to find people who were just as isolated and desperate as we were. We became part of a larger group of gay men and lesbians who did not want to go on suffering the disaster of addiction. This wish became a bond that linked us together no matter how isolated we continued to feel when we returned to our own rooms or houses.

There seems little doubt that meetings *saved* our lives. It was in these meetings, however, that we learned about the tools that *changed* our lives. As we struggled with our disease, we discovered we could rely on these tools to get us through any ordeal we needed to face. This complete sequence of Steps we have used to create the foundation for understanding ourselves and the world in recovery is recapitulated in Step Twelve; "Having had a spiritual awakening *as the result of these steps. . .*" Because it is an omnibus Step, one that depends on the effects of other Steps, exploring some of the linkages developed through the Steps preceding it is valuable.

Connecting the Steps

One of the most obvious connections is the relationship between Steps One, Two, and Three and Step Twelve. The journey into recovery could never have begun unless we accepted our predicament as addicts and made ourselves available to help. This required acceptance, faith and surrender. The struggle to submit ourselves to these is the story of our wilderness days, when our addiction seemed so tempting and powerful that we wondered if we would ever have strength enough to let it go. Unless we have worked, and continue to work, on these basic Steps, we go nowhere in our journey.

With the support of the group, many of us made it through the beginning Steps. The group helped us to overcome our denial, our sense of hopelessness, and our insistence upon our own willfulness. The effect on us of these first three basic Steps of the program made it possible for us to begin to change our lives.

Until we had done them, we were not ready for Step Four, which required intensive focus on ourselves. Only after the change process was begun were we prepared to develop a "fearless" and "thorough" moral inventory of ourselves. It was only then we experienced the beginning of a new kind of intervention that allowed us to know we no longer had to do anything alone, that there was help for us. This was the growing awareness that we relied on when we faced our secrets and identified the obstacles recorded in our inventory. Sharing this inventory with another human being, *and with our Higher Power*, we spoke in our own voice about the unspeakable. To our amazement, we survived! Step Five was not the end of the world, even though we behaved as if it would be.

In addition to the facing and sharing of our secrets, this Step was a leap forward in relating in a different way to another human being. In the process of trusting someone else, we discovered that we were not abandoned or cast out because of the enormity of our shortcomings, nor were we alone in our vulnerability and imperfection. On this foundation of another person's acceptance, we began to build the bridge to *self-acceptance* that had never been there in our alcoholic lives as gay men and lesbians.

As we gradually link together the work we do in Steps Five, Nine, and Twelve, we begin to develop an ever-widening circle of acceptance. With the second inventory that we made in Step Eight, in Step Nine we reach out to make amends to all those we have harmed. These are the people from our past who have played a major role in our lives and account for much of the way we feel about ourselves. Through making amends to them, we accept responsibility for our previous actions and begin creating the honesty and trust in others that had always been missing. By willingly taking this reponsibility on ourselves, we begin forging new links in the chain of *self-trust* and *self-caring*.

Through these amends, as well as those we continue to make, we are able to see that no one holds the reins of our recovery except ourselves. Unless we are absolutely clear about this, we slip back into old addictive habits of dependency in which new people we meet fill old needs that threaten our recovery.

It is in Step Twelve that the circle expands to include everyone in our lives—those in a program, those not in a program, those to whom we have made or still owe amends, and those with whom we have a clean slate. By this time, we understand the role we have played in choosing everyone who has a significant role in our lives. We become aware that from now on we must carefully and consistently consider our priorities in recovery. We need also to remember how vitally important these priorities are to our continued progress.

Haven't people always been an enigma for us? In our addiction, we have looked for affirmation and for love from the very ones who were least able to give it. By taking responsibility for our choices, in Step Nine, we provide ourselves with the information we need to guide us as we meet new people we can trust and who can support us. It is only with the honesty and trust in ourselves that comes through Steps Five and Nine that we can begin to use new patterns of thought and action to interact with the people around us. For us to connect with others in the enlightened way that Step Twelve describes, we must have laid this foundation.

Perhaps of all the paradoxes in Twelve-Step programs, the most basic is that we must give away our recovery in order to keep it.

Only through sharing with others what we have received by working the Steps is it possible to hold onto these benefits. In this activity of sharing, we become the source of support for others as we carry the message of the program to them. The willingness to do this becomes the key to our own recovery as we continue the journey.

That we have important work to do, that others depend on us to do it, that we need them as much as they need us are among the most amazing discoveries we make in our journey. What a paradox! It is only by being a member of a group that we can experience ourselves in a way that never seemed possible before. And what a revelation it is to begin now to understand that we are more *like* other people, gay or straight, than we are *unlike* them! Participation as an equal with everyone else is, for some of us, tantamount to a "spiritual awakening." Most gay men and lesbians never thought such an experience possible! With it, we are able, once and for all, to end the imprisoning isolation of our uniqueness and participate in life in the same way we see others participating.

This experience of ourselves as members of a group helps us to begin to examine some old ideas that have always motivated our thoughts and actions. For the first time, we observe that everyone does not take the same things for granted or use the same rules we do. We see that there are many more choices available than we ever believed. Through the Steps, we are able to put our old behavior into perspective and discover we are capable of change instead of being fixed entities. While this is happening, the group around us provides us with the opportunity to dump the wreckage of the past and create the space in which to make new connections inside ourselves.

As we clear away old patterns of thought and behavior and replace them with healthy new ones we develop through the Steps, the space within us expands. It is this expanding space, this availability within each of us that opens in the process of recovery, that is the focus of the last three Steps of the program.

Each of these Steps is about relationship and our level of consciousness. The linkage between them is important for us to consider. Each Step is concerned with raising our consciousness about ourselves (Ten), our consciousness about our relationship with a Higher Power (Eleven), and our consciousness about our relationship with others in the world around us (Twelve). It is with new insights arising from honesty and trust, instead of our old, addictive patterns, that we are now capable of creating and developing relationships. These new relationships become the basis for living happy, healthy lives in recovery.

We are on the main road of the journey into sobriety when we search for the answers to the following questions:

- What efforts will we make to develop our relationship with ourselves, with a Higher Power, with others?
- Will we expand our emotional, intellectual and spiritual limits or maintain them as they are?
- What are the real challenges waiting for us in recovery?

No one has the answers to any of these questions the first, second, or even the third time through the Steps. What we do have is the awareness that these questions are there for us to work on with the tools of the program.

Practicing the Principles

Being capable of having a different relationship with ourselves, with a Higher Power, and with the world around us does not mean that we will have one. We have to make a consistent, conscious effort. The tenth Step inventory, and the need for prayer and meditation suggested by the eleventh Step are examples of this exceptional kind of effort. The twelfth Step suggests a *third* kind of effort we must make if we are going to create a new relationship with the world: "to carry this message to alcoholics, and to practice these principles in all our affairs."

This is strenuous work! The alternative to taking this action, unfortunately, is that we may find ourselves back again on the other side of the door. That door swings both ways, and for some alcoholics who find themselves in and out of the program every few months, it becomes a revolving door. Any of us can go through it as many times as we choose; some of us, however, cannot find this door again once we are outside.

Is this effort we must make really such a burden? Remember that we were invited to return after our first meeting in order to participate in the work of recovery. Given the state of collapse we were in, many of us could hardly believe the invitation. Nevertheless, we took our seats beside others with whom we gradually became more comfortable. We found relief from our pain and discovered that they did too. It is important to remember that it was not through silence, indifference, or "stuffing it," but through the effort to share our pain and suffering that relief came. Healing began only as we exposed our wounds and our anguish.

In the process of sharing with others just like ourselves, we were able to change our perspective on everything. We became a witness to our agony, and as we listened to others, we shared in their witness. There is a striking similarity between this and the recitation that Christians and Jews practice in reading from the Bible through the liturgical calendar. The prophets and the gospel writers were also witnesses to disaster, triumph, tragedy, sorrow, affliction, persecution, defeat, and the entire gamut of human experience. Men and women through the centuries have taken hope, faith, strength and joy for their own lives from the accounts they left. The recitations of these witnesses have consistently raised individual consciousness beyond the personal into an awareness of the human condition. In some vital way, the account of any witness changes the course of history.

We change our own individual history when we walk into any Twelve-Step program. Witnessing changes our lives. Through it, we come to realize that each one is not only a member of the group in which we share, but also a loving member of the human race, not an outcast! This is diametrically opposite from the way we lived in our addiction. We are no longer victims; all of us have our experience, strength and hope to witness, and these are valuable to us and to others. Each story confirms this, for we learn from others how to make important connections that have been missing in our lives. Each story binds us all together in a chain of recovery that works to support every one of us. We become participants in community and recognize that we are important to life.

Until we, as gay men and lesbians, have accepted ourselves as members (along with the responsibility of membership) of the community in recovery, we remain outsiders looking at happiness like children in front of a candy store window. We see what is there on the other side of the pane, but we cannot touch or taste it. This deprivation can grow and become the source of bitter suffering.

Recovering from the effects of the disease of alcoholism with the help of the Steps is the first task we must undertake. Given the nature of the disease, this is an ongoing effort. But the journey continues, with the help of the Steps, into recovering into life. For us, this means that we must continue to work on changing the rules we thought we needed in order to survive. No matter how committed we have been to any of them, we must be willing to grow beyond them. "If you change even one thing, you change everything." None of us understands how significant this truth about living is until he or she sets out on the journey to recovery.

In recovery, we discover that we cannot share our lives with those around us without learning honesty, nor can we continue listening to others share their lives without learning acceptance. Next, we discover that the gaping abyss left when we stopped using all mood-altering substances gets filled when we begin to work the Steps instead of pursuing our self-will. With honesty, acceptance, and the Steps, we finally discover the way to begin developing a connection between our heads and our hearts that had never been possible in the compartmentalized life most of us led as gay men and lesbians in a straight society.

The "Spiritual Awakening"

Because the Steps provide us with the tools we need to help us connect with ourselves, it becomes possible for us to connect with other people exactly the way they are instead of the way we may wish or want them to be. The desperate pursuit of perfection that motivated our lives is transformed in this process. When we search for something we consider beyond us, we will never find what we seek. By looking within ourselves, we learn the way to love what is—instead of what isn't.

Many of us truly believed we had taken a giant step beyond childhood when we first discovered what it was like to get "high." Instead of growing up, thousands of us found our way into addiction and got stuck there. We were never capable of developing a deep personal connection with anyone around us because of the substances we depended on. When we enter recovery, however, we begin learning to connect as individuals who are capable of evolving. We discover that we can find happiness, joy and freedom in a world in which we knew only despair. *That* is the giant step that is waiting for us in recovery.

No one could have told us when we began this journey the place we would reach, how far we would travel or with whom. From where we stand now, we should be able to see that we could not have arrived at this moment unless we had come through all the other moments along the way. Like many other answers that have found their way into our lives, this one reveals itself as we live through the journey: *we can only get here from there!* We reach this place in our recovery because we have consciously made efforts to use our energy through each experience that led us to it.

Three times in recovery I have gone to Yosemite National Park, and each time I have marveled at the effects of a prehistoric geological devastation that radically altered the mountains and valleys of that corner of California. On my second visit, I went to Glacier Point and looked into the valley three thousand feet below. Seeing the majesty of Half Dome rise across the way in the midst of its rocky wilderness, I realized that seen from the perspective of time and distance, there is great beauty in nature's scars. As I stood looking with wonder at those massive peaks and plunging chasms, and the space they are set in, I understood that it would not be the miracle it is now without the disaster that overtook it all those millennia ago.

If we are willing to be taught, nature constantly provides us with valuable insights. For many of us, these insights are the basis of the "spiritual awakening" referred to in Step Twelve. The realization that we are each remarkable *because* we have endured the devastation of addiction, and the daily struggle with recovery, comes only with time and distance in the journey itself. This understanding was not there when we started out; our pain and our suffering were all that we knew. All of us are healed by our willingness to pass beyond our suffering, and we learn this again and again through Step Twelve.

Thousands of gay and lesbian alcoholics are out there in the world around us cut off from life and dying from addiction. None of them has any idea that help is even possible. Those of us who are learning to find our way have each other to help us. We all need to remember that carrying this message to others is essential to our own journey into recovery.

"Will it save lives?" asked Bill W. when asked for his approval for gay AA meetings in Boston in the early 1950s. As a member of this ever-expanding community in recovery, it is up to you to discover whether or not it saves *your* life—as well as the lives of others. There is help for gay and lesbian alcoholics everywhere. These twelve Steps of recovery are waiting for us to find them, and use them. "The program works, if you work it!"

GUIDES TO PROGRESS

Christmas, 1984: It is snowing briskly and there is just enough of it now on the ground to cover the dark earth. The sky is Maine gray. A great stuffed horned owl sits on the television set across the room, and country and western music waltzes around the Christmas tree. I sit in a living room with people I met only yesterday. That is strange—to spend Christmas with total strangers in a totally strange place. Is is very different from last year when I was alone in a familiar place. Since then, I've made a lot of progress with my recovery, and I've become very patient with myself and everyone else. The picture window through which I look opens on a scene of clump birch, a white house with black shutters, and a street without a sidewalk. New England is everywhere around me, and new friends are wrapping presents in the next room. How curious it was to go shopping this morning without money. Somehow, the matter of need became paramount. What is paramount in anything? I think being sober to experience being human is paramount. The wish to be totally who I am and to connect totally with others exactly as they are is paramount. (Excerpted from author's journal)

First, she had a bad dream about her father. Then, she lost her wallet. The cold she had last week was getting worse, and the project that had to be completed by Friday was still sitting in her drawer. Joan was beginning to play some old tapes from the past about what a loser she was and how foolish it was to try to change her life after twenty years of drinking. Instead of going on with that kind of thinking, she got out her list of AA telephone numbers and called the first one. The voice she heard on the other end was a recording, but it was exactly the message she needed to hear: "Hi there, how's it going? The rest of the world doesn't have a Twelve-Step program, but *we* do. Aren't we lucky? Think about it, and tell me what's up with you, and I'll get back to you in a little while." Joan left her name and number, hung up the phone, and did a brief gratitude inventory of the good things that had happened to her since she began in recovery. She had to agree; she really was lucky.

Suggestions for Action

Whether you go to mainstream meetings or gay and lesbian meetings, look for similarities between you and other people instead of focusing on the differences. Remember, we are more *like* other people than we are different.

REFLECTIONS

Living the miracle—that is our work. When we understand what we have been given and the possibilities that are ours through this gift, we are present to the miracle—our own miracle.

EPILOGUE

No matter where we are in the Twelve-Step cycle, recovery is an ongoing process in which each day is always the beginning. If we are honest with ourselves about the nature of the disease, we are always *recovering* and never *recovered* from it.

After we tasted our first sip of alcohol, and decided that we liked it—or liked what it did for us—we did it again . . . and again. Having journeyed through the Twelve Steps, having had our first experience of affirming and supporting ourselves with love, validation, honesty, fellowship, it is up to us to continue the same process, and work at it again . . . and again. We always have the choice, and if we like what happens in our lives when we work at recovering, these Steps continue to provide us with an ever-unfolding road map to go on with the journey.

We often forget that no one except ourselves can always love us in precisely the way we want and need to be loved. Loving ourselves takes practice, and time. We hear, from time to time, that people in Twelve-Step programs love us until we can learn to love ourselves. The experience of this love can fill us with both pride and humility, for it means that we have become valuable members of the human family. As members, we embrace each other for exactly who we are, the way we are. This is tremendously freeing because it provides us with a place to stand on and accept ourselves. It is the place from which our mountains are moved and our new lives begun.

Embracing Diversity in Community

There is tremendous energy in the power of love. Participants in Twelve-Step programs grow in understanding of this energy and its relationship with health. As we go on in recovery, what we are becomes the basis for continuing growth and development. We integrate our diversity more and more and, at the same time, learn to appreciate each of the parts more deeply. It is the experience of wholeness and well-being within ourselves—and within society, and the universe—that extends our concept of who we are and what we mean to others. Recovery is the reentry into the heart of humanity.

We are survivors of the devastation of addiction. We know many who are still suffering from the ravages of the disease, and we are right to feel lucky and grateful. Many of us joined the fellowship of the Twelve-Step programs as isolated gay men and lesbians; now we have become part of a community. Through our participation in this community, we express our individuality. It's a paradox: only by expressing our individuality do we actually become a member of the community.

In mobilizing against the AIDS crisis, the gay community has shown the way to a deep and humanitarian response to suffering and social ostracism. The hospices and home-care projects are models for a humane, responsible, loving initiative that has made the lives of many who have fallen ill from this disease much easier to bear. The gay community has reached out to embrace the exiles, and because of this action, the gay community has grown in love and understanding.

In the gay and lesbian meetings of the Twelve-Step programs, the entire spectrum of individual diversity is accepted. Embracing the diversity that exists within the gay community itself might, in the future, become the model of acceptance for *all* gay men and *all* lesbians whether they are substance-addicted or not. Just as the Twelve-Step programs have provided a new concept of fellowship and group participation throughout the world, so this same impulse for the acceptance of gay and lesbian diversity *by* the gay and lesbian community seems a possibility waiting in the wings for this century.

We need first to accept our gay brothers and lesbian sisters ourselves before we expect the rest of the world to do so. Is it not possible that after *our* acceptance, the rest will follow? This is what has happened with alcoholics and addicts over the past half-century of Twelve-Step programs! First the alcoholics and addicts welcomed each other into their own fellowship, and then the rest of society followed their lead.

The Longest Journey

We are all on an amazing journey. We have come many miles and years through space and time, through the mind and the heart, on the journey back into life. Back again in life, we encounter the reality of our gayness, our virtue, and our merit as men and women who can be lovers—man to man, woman to woman. Is this important? Is it important to write a book about recovering into life as a gay man and as a lesbian? Yes, because being gay is important to us!

We have laughed and cried, alone and with others, at the wonderful insights and revelations that have come to us as we traveled. We have also known the miracle of being with those who love us because we shared our vulnerability with them. I believe that we have been made richer in understanding and experienced gratitude much deeper than we ever believed possible. I know I have. Many of us have lived through the incredible paradox that the disasters that befell us were the very ones we needed to grow through in order to discover the meaning of happiness.

As members of the community, we know we have the right to as much joy and freedom as anyone else. As sober, proud, and responsible gay men and lesbians who touch other people's lives with the richness of our diversity today and every day, we continue our journey together. Wishing everyone the joy of the journey, I hope we may all meet along the way to celebrate our gifts and the gift-givers.

APPENDIX A

The Signs of Alcoholism/Addiction

	Yes	No
1. Do you occasionally drink or use drugs after a disappointment, a quarrel, or when the boss gives you a hard time?	✓	
2. When you have trouble or feel under pressure, do you always drink or use more heavily than usual?	✓	
3. Have you noticed that you are able to handle more liquor or other mood-altering substances than you did when you first began?	✓	
4. Did you ever wake up the "morning after" and discover that you could not remember part of the evening before, even though your friends tell you that you did not "pass out"?	✓	
5. When drinking or using with other people, do you try to get in a few extra ones when others will not notice?		✓
6. Are there certain occasions when you feel uncomfortable if alcohol or mood-altering substances are not available?	✓	
7. Have you recently noticed that when you begin drinking or using you are more in a hurry to get the first one than you used to be?	✓	

	Yes	No
8. Do you sometimes feel a little guilty about your drinking or using?	✓	
9. Are you secretly irritated when your family or friends discuss your drinking or using?	Not Any more	
10. Have you often found that you wish to continue drinking or using after your friends say they have had enough?	✓	
11. Do you usually have a reason for the occasions when you drink or use heavily?	✓	✓
12. Have you recently noticed an increase in the frequency of your memory "blackouts"?		
13. When you are sober, do you often regret things you have done or said while drinking or using?	✓	
14. Have you tried switching brands or substances, or following different plans for controlling your drinking or using?	✓	
15. Have you often failed to keep the promises you have made to yourself about controlling or cutting down on your drinking or using?	✓	
16. Have you ever tried to control your drinking or using by making a change in jobs or moving to a new location?	✓	
17. Do you try to avoid family or close friends while you are drinking or using?	✓	
18. Are you having an increasing number of financial and work problems?	✓	
19. Do more people seem to be treating you unfairly without good reasons?		✓
20. Do you eat very little or irregularly when you are drinking?	✓	

Yes   No

21. Do you sometimes have the "shakes" in the morning and find that it helps to have a little "pick-me-up"? ___ ✓

22. Have you recently noticed that you cannot drink or use as much as you once did? ✓ ___

23. Do you sometimes stay under the influence of alcohol or drugs for several days at a time? ✓ ___

24. Do you sometimes feel very depressed and wonder whether life is worth living? ✓ ___

25. Sometimes after periods of drinking or using, do you see or hear things that aren't there? ✓ ___

26. Do you get terribly frightened after you have been drinking or using drugs heavily? ✓ ___

If you answered yes to any of the questions, you have some of the symptoms that may indicate alcoholism or addiction to other mood-altering substances. Yes answers to several of the questions indicate the following stages of alcoholism or addiction: Questions 1–8, early stage; questions 9–21, middle stage; questions 22–26, the beginning of the final stage.

Checklist adapted from the National Council on Alcoholism, "What Are the Signs?"

APPENDIX B

Indications of Co-dependency

Have you ever

1. Been embarrassed at the behavior of someone you know after he or she drinks or uses mood-altering substances?

2. Disposed of alcohol or substances to keep someone from using them?

3. Felt your behvior was making someone else drink or use?

4. Threatened to leave someone because of too much drinking or using of mood-altering substances?

5. Called work to give an excuse for someone who could not work that day because of excessive alcohol or substance abuse the day or night before?

6. Felt angry that the basic necessities of life were not being taken care of because so much money was being spent on alcohol or mood-altering substances?

7. Felt fearful at what would happen to your and/or others dependent upon you if drinking or using continues in your relationship/family?

8. Left home to look for someone who you think might be out drinking or using?

9. Called bars, neighbors, friends, looking for someone you believe is either drinking or using?

10. Increased your own consumption of alcohol or substances in order to keep up with someone who is a heavy drinker or user?

11. Wished that alcohol or mood-altering substances could be outlawed?

12. Wanted to move and "start over" as a solution to the drinking and/or drug-use problem going on around you?

13. Been revolted by others' drinking/using behavior?

14. Been unable to sleep because someone has stayed out late drinking or using drugs or not come home at all?

15. Resented that there is heavy drinking or drug use going on in the life of someone close to you?

16. Felt hopeless about a substance-abuse situation?

17. Felt it was a disgrace, or that it was simply not possible to talk about a drinking or drug abuse problem?

18. Cut down on activities outside your own home in order to keep an eye on someone who is drinking or using drugs?

19. Complained, nagged, or got into quarrels with someone who drinks or uses drugs?

20. Felt that if the substance abuser would just stop, everything would be okay?

Adapted from a checklist developed by the National Council on Alcoholism–Bay Area.

RESOURCES

Recovery Literature

Alcoholics Anonymous. New York: Alcoholics Anonymous World Services, 1976.

Beattie, Melody. *Codependent No More*. San Francisco: Harper & Row, 1987.

Black, Claudia. *It Will Never Happen to Me!* Denver: M.A.C. Printing and Publications Division, 1982.

Carnes, Patrick. *The Sexual Addiction*. Minneapolis: CompCare Publications, 1983.

Cermak, Timmon L. *A Time to Heal*. Los Angeles: Jeremy P. Tarcher, Inc., 1988.

Delaney, M. and P. Goldblum. *Strategies for Survival*. New York, St. Martin's Press, 1987.

Living Sober. New York: Alcoholics Anonymous World Services, 1975.

Schaef, Anne W. *When Society Becomes an Addict*. San Francisco: Harper & Row, 1987.

Swallow, Jean, ed., *Out From Under: Sober Dykes and Our Friends*. San Francisco: Spinsters, Ink, 1983.

Twelve Steps and Twelve Traditions. New York: Alcoholics Anonymous World Services, 1952, 1953, 1981.

Wegscheider-Cruse, Sharon. *Choicemaking*. Pompano Beach, FL: Health Communications, 1985.

Woititz, Janet, G. *Adult Children of Alcoholics*. Pompano Beach, FL: Health Communications, 1983.

The Gay and Lesbian Experience

Borhek, Mary. *Coming Out to Parents*. New York: Pilgrim Press, 1983.

Clark, Don. *Loving Someone Gay*. New York: Signet, 1977.

Fortunato, John. *Embracing the Exile: Healing Journeys of Gay Christians.* San Francisco: Harper & Row, 1982.

_____. *AIDS: The Spiritual Dilemma,* San Francisco: Harper & Row, 1987.

Silverstein, Charles. *Man to Man.* New York: Quill, 1982.

Wolfe, Susan J., and Julia P. Stanley, eds. *The Coming Out Stories.* Watertown, MA: Persephone Press, 1980.

Spirituality

Buber, Martin. *I and Thou.* New York: Charles Scribner's Sons, 1958.

Kopp, Shelden. *An End to Innocence.* New York: Bantam, 1978.

_____. *If You Meet the Buddha on the Road, Kill Him!* New York: Bantam, 1976.

Lindbergh, Anne Morrow. *Gift from the Sea.* New York: Random House, 1955.

Teilhard de Chardin, Pierre. *The Phenomenon of Man.* Trans. by Bernard Wall. New York: Harper & Row, 1959, 1961, 1965.